'From passion to persist
through the five essent
looking for top-notch tips, exceptional tools and real-time
success stories that will grow and transform your fundraising
program to better serve your crucial mission.'

Martha H. Schumacher, CFRE, ACFRE,
MInstF, President, Hazen and HILT

'Bernard and Clare present us with a simple and perfect guide
to do a successful solicitation in our major campaigns. This
is a book that every fundraiser will learn from and enjoy.'

Isabella Navarro, Vice President for Whole Person
Education, UDEM University, Monterrey, Mexico

'Wow – a FANTASTIC collection of 20 power tools to transform a fundraiser's ability to ask major donors for major
funds. I'm already applying them to my work with clients,
and sharing them with my students.'

Liz Ngonzi, Executive Director, The International Social Impact
Institute; Adjunct Assistant Professor, New York City University

'At a time of huge uncertainty and ambiguity and when charitable income has rarely been under more pressure, along
comes this essential read, packed with thoughtful insights
and practical tips that will enhance any fundraiser's ability to
make a compelling and impactful ask for a major gift.'

Paul Amadi OBE, Chief Supporter Officer,
British Red Cross

'Once again, Bernard and Clare have put together an essential book for those working with high net worth individuals,

based on their vast research and experience. The inspiring examples and the practical tools to make a successful ask will guide you to brilliant results in any culture or country, regardless of how big your organisation is or whether your cause is "difficult".'

Norma Galafassi, Director, in2action.net, South America; past Chair, Argentinian Association of Fundraisers

'To get money to achieve your mission, you need to ask people for donations. Ross and Segal's super new book, *Making the Ask*, combines years of proven experience with decision science to give you practical and applicable tools to make the ask. It engagingly breaks down how to prepare your propositions passionately and persuasively for success. Read it. Practise the tools, and you will make the ask better and raise more money.'

Marina Jones, Head of Membership and Fundraising Appeals, Royal Opera House

'Whether you are a novice to the major gift universe or an accomplished and experienced fundraiser, Clare Segal and Bernard Ross' compelling 5Ps framework with 20 practical tools will change the way you perceive your donors and ultimately make your relationship-building approach more effective… and successful. There is great learning in this book for everyone! And I will definitely make it a mandatory reading for my Major Gift Officers.'

Thomas Kurmann, Vice President of Resource Development, Oxfam USA

'Fundraising is about asking. *Making the Ask* by Bernard Ross and Clare Segal is such a powerful book not only for major donor fundraisers but all fundraisers. In over 40 years of fundraising experience, I have read many fundraising books and only a few have made me feel better skilled at doing fundraising at the end of reading them. *Making the Ask* is such a book. I love the 5Ps, which are both easy to remember and very practical. I highly recommend this book, especially if you want to be a better fundraiser.'

Leo Orland, FFIA CFRE, Past Chair,
Fundraising Institute of Australia

'*Making the Ask* is a brilliant guide and a must-read for all major gift fundraisers, especially in Asia where HNWIs philanthropy is experiencing rapid growth. This is an amazing work.'

Masataka Uo, CEO, Japan Fundraising Association

'A powerful, practical and enlightening book that is packed with fundraising nuggets! It will leave you fired up and raring to go. Definitely the best fundraising book I have read in years.'

Naholi Mike Muchilwa, Author and Founder of
the Kenya Association of Fundraising Professionals

'Unfortunately the non-profits in emerging markets are still not practising strategic major gift fundraising. Often, this is because of a gap in knowledge and skills to prospect, approach and ask. This book can help fill that gap and motivate small, mid-size and even large charities to derive the most value for their extremely precious causes.'

Anup Tiwari, Board Member,
South Asian Fundraising Group; International
Representative, SOS Children's Villages International

'The techniques presented by Ross and Segal in *Making the Ask* offer an exciting deep dive into the science of fundraising, providing insight into the mindset of every type of donor – including the vital HNWI supporters.'

Houssam Chahin, Chief of Private Sector Partnerships for UNHCR, MENA

'This is a must-read orientation on behavioural science and how it can radically improve your fundraising performance. If you want to transform your major gift fundraising and create deep and lasting relationships with your donors, *Making the Ask* is an essential read.'

Anne-Marie Gray, CEO, USA for UNHCR

'Bernard and Clare just 'get' fundraising. Their advice is based on research, evidence and practice, and explained in an accessible format. Every fundraiser, regardless of sector and experience, should read this book and keep it in their fundraising toolbox.'

Susan Fisher, former Director of Development at the Science Museum London, now Director of Development at English Heritage

We are grateful for these generous endorsements, which are all in a personal capacity.

Making
the
Ask

THE ARTFUL SCIENCE
OF HIGH-VALUE
FUNDRAISING

Bernard Ross & Clare Segal

First published in Great Britain by Practical Inspiration Publishing, 2021

© Bernard Ross and Clare Segal, 2021

The moral rights of the authors have been asserted.

ISBN   9781788602372 (print)
       9781788602365 (epub)
       9781788602358 (mobi)

Every effort has been made to trace copyright holders and to obtain their permission for the use of copyright material. The publisher apologizes for any errors or omissions and would be grateful if notified of any corrections that should be incorporated in future reprints or editions of this book.

Practical Inspiration
Publishing

To Kathleen Liddell Hart – a truly
inspirational woman.

Contents

Preface...*xi*

Making the ask: 20 power tools.........................xvii

Chapter 1: Passion.. 1
Tool 1: Create a powerful emotional anchor 6
Tool 2: Establish your personal brand..........................14
Tool 3: Create a philanthropic PIN code 20
Tool 4: DOSE the prospect – become a donor
     drug dealer! 33

Chapter 2: Proposal...................................... 41
Tool 5: Build an =mc story arc 46
Tool 6: Hold out for a hero 56
Tool 7: Price your philanthropic propositions.................62
Tool 8: Check for (sticky) SUCCESS...........................74

Chapter 3: Preparation 93
Tool 9: Develop a well-formed outcome 96
Tool 10: Set out your LIM-its.....................................108
Tool 11: Flexibly reframe..114
Tool 12: Link think, feel, do 131

Chapter 4: Persuasion 139
Tool 13: Try philanthropic pre-suasion –
     prime for success...141
Tool 14: Pay absolute attention with the silent listen 149
Tool 15: Build rapid rapport......................................158
Tool 16: Match language style – switch sensory
     systems...172

Chapter 5: Persistence... **187**

Tool 17: Pivot perceptual positions – choose
        another angle..189

Tool 18: Anticipate killer questions 204

Tool 19: Call your mental mentors – ask for help 208

Tool 20: Manage the nine fundraising 'no's 213

Final summary... and bonus tool
21: Ask three questions... **221**

Books and online resources...................................... **225**

Acknowledgements..235

Preface

Over 10 years ago, we wrote a book called *The Influential Fundraiser*. It introduced a new model for influence that we'd developed to help fundraisers and others working for social good to increase their effectiveness. For the first time, it used the sciences of neurology and psychology to transform the way fundraisers approach their work. In the process it became a bestseller, and since then the model has been used successfully by fundraisers not only in the established markets of Europe and the United States, but also in Ethiopia, Brazil, Mexico, Australia, Thailand, India, China and many other countries and cultures. It has been used successfully across a range of philanthropic fields – arts and culture, higher education, environmental causes, healthcare, social justice, social enterprise and international development.

This new book does something different. It focuses on the business of approaching high net worth individuals (HNWI), either one-to-one or in small group settings. It builds on a decade of experimentation, practical use and feedback. And it focuses more directly on one of the scariest aspects of fundraising – actually *making the ask*. We've organised it round 20 powerful tools to improve your ability to ask for funds and be successful – whether it's online or in person, and for £10,000 or £10 million. It also builds on the science we knew then and brings in developments and insights from disciplines such as behavioural economics, neuroscience and evolutionary psychology.

We've taken the opportunity while working on this book to test some new approaches with our brave customers. We're delighted to have helped and been helped by the following organisations:

- *Diane Fossey Gorilla Fund (DFGF)*. The fund wanted to build a specialist conservation and education centre to protect the last 750 mountain gorillas in Rwanda. We coached the president of DFGF to make successful US$1 million+ solicitations to several wealthy philanthropists, including billionaires Ted Turner and Larry Ellison.

- *KidsOR*. This is a charity building a paediatric surgical unit and aiming to train surgeons, nurses and anaesthetists in every African nation by 2030. It needs US$100 million over the next five years from major donors in Africa and further afield – we developed the strategy and used our learning to shape their powerful case for support.

- *UNHCR*. We worked with a specialist team based in Dubai, which has to raise more than US$300 million every year across the Middle East to meet the growing needs of refugees. We combined our *Making the Ask* techniques with Islamic philanthropic principles to create a convincing framework.

- *British Heart Foundation*. We trained the chair and volunteer board of this major UK health charity to improve their ability and confidence to ask wealthy peers for their financial support. They gained confidence by using many of the tools discussed here.

- *Stonewall*. This UK-based campaigning equality agency offered to train 20 leading Southern African LGBTQI+ activists to make fundraising asks for a cause that is often dangerous or difficult to even mention in some repressive nations. The tools we offered enabled them to frame their ideas effectively, challenging prejudices.

- *University of Glasgow*. The university launched its first £1 billion campaign and wanted to make sure the whole development team were both on board and had the new skills and confidence they needed. We were delighted to teach those skills and build their discipline and shared approach.

We would like to thank these agencies and the many hundreds of others who took part in our extensive field trials of the approaches we've outlined here.

The insights on how to be successful described in *Making the Ask* are based primarily on a distillation of our practical experience as management consultants, coaches and fundraisers working in the not-for-profit world through our company, mc consulting. We're also happy to acknowledge that we've built on the work of others. If you are familiar with behavioural science, social psychology and personal development, you'll recognise that we've drawn knowledge and learning from:

- *Psychology*. We've selected strategies from a range of approaches, from cognitive behaviour therapy (CBT) to neuro-linguistic programming (NLP). These disciplines offer profound insights into the way people make choices.

- *Social anthropology.* We've drawn on the body language work of Albert Mehrabian and Alan Pease, both of whom have informed our thinking on building rapport.

- *Therapy.* We've been hugely influenced by the late Milton Erickson, especially his skills and insights on empathetic matching and pacing.

- *Academic research.* In particular, we have used Cialdini's research on influence and Dan Ariely's work on human irrationality.

If you want to dive even deeper into any of these topics see the Resources list at the end of the book and the website we've created at mc.consulting/makingtheask.

We must give a special shout-out to Daniel Kahneman, whose book *Thinking Fast and Slow*[1] first introduced us to behavioural science. He gave us the courage to put aside much of the formal rational business-case thinking that influenced a great deal of our early work on influence and decisions – and that continues to affect much fundraising thinking.

Kahneman's model of System 1 and System 2 decision-making subtly informs much of this book and the 20 tools we introduce. From his work, we now know everyone's brain is fundamentally lazy, and will look for the simplest, fastest, easiest answer to any question or choice. To put it more politely, the unwritten law of least effort means we are predisposed to take mental shortcuts. We all use these

---

[1] Daniel Kahneman, *Thinking Fast and Slow* (2011).

shortcuts – technically called heuristics – to help us save mental energy[2] and get to an answer. The key learning for fundraisers is that donors or prospects – would-be donors – want us to ask them for support in the simplest, easiest way possible.

The 20 tools featured in this book are based on practical, real-world approaches that have been tested in tough fundraising situations. Some, like a screwdriver, you can use straight out of the toolbox; others need a lot of practice. Used well and appropriately, they can help you share complex ideas simply, connect quickly to nervous or anxious donors, and build deeper relationships with existing supporters.

As always, we're keen to keep learning. We'd love to hear what works for you and how we can improve our approach. If you have ideas or feedback, or want to contact us to enquire about training or coaching, let us know at bernardross@mc.consulting or claresegal@mc.consulting.

Enjoy the book. And more, enjoy the success we hope it will bring to your important work.

---

[2] The reason behind this laziness is that while it constitutes just 2% of total body weight, the brain uses 20% of total energy consumption measured in blood circulation. There is a good physiological reason why our ancestors learned this 'minimum effort' approach.

Making the ask:
20 power tools

We thought you might find a quick overview of the book's key ideas useful. Strap in!

Our approach assumes there are five key stages to making a successful ask – sometimes technically called a solicitation – for a major gift. These are:

1. *Passion:* getting yourself and the prospect into the best possible mental and emotional state to take the risk involved in making a big ask to an exceptionally wealthy individual.

2. *Proposal:* organising your thoughts and organisational need into an attractive package that will appeal to the prospect.[1]

3. *Preparation:* thinking through the implications of different options about how to present your ideas to the prospect.

4. *Persuasion:* the business of actually making the ask in a room, at a cultivation event, over the phone or on Zoom, or even in an email.

---

[1] 'Prospect' is the word we'll use throughout the book to mean an individual who you've identified as potentially able and willing to make a significant gift to your cause.

5. *Persistence:* a way to review how your ask went, learn from it and, where appropriate, try to re-engage the prospect.

We think about these five stages as an element in the bigger and longer supporter journey – from 'acquisition' of the prospect to 'stewardship' after you've received a gift. That process is part of a bigger book. We've focused here on making a first ask to a prospect. Once successful, your relationship – based, we hope, on mutual trust, respect and understanding – should be your primary way of engaging with any prospect.

You'll notice that within each stage there are four tools. Altogether, this gives you a toolkit of 20 powerful tried and tested, guaranteed-to-work approaches to solve any problem you might face in your ask. All the tools draw on the emerging sciences of behavioural economics, neuroscience and evolutional psychology. Some will be familiar to professional fundraisers. A number will be brand new and may challenge what is viewed as conventional 'best practice'. A few may even appear counter-intuitive. However, do bear in mind that they have been *proven* to work in a range of settings, for a range of single gifts up to £50 million and in a range of cultures and countries.

The approach we outline in the following chapters concentrates on asking in person, but you'll find that many also work across a range of communication channels – formal written proposals, email, phone and of course video calls through Zoom, Skype, etc.

Top tip: The 100% successful ask

We've written the very best book we can, with the very best ideas and tools. But the fundamental secret to the 100% successful ask remains the same. It's all about the three 'bests':

- The *best approach* to fundraising from a high value individual – or any prospect – is always face to face. This means you see all the feedback and impact in real time and can respond to it.

- The *best person* to make a high value ask is an *existing donor* – someone who's shown commitment already – to a *peer who is a prospect* and *with whom they have a relationship and a shared set of values.*

- The *best gift level* is from an existing donor asking for a gift from that peer at roughly the same level at which they gave. Bill Gates asking you for £10,000 feels a bit off; similarly, a £10,000 donor asking Bill for £10,000 would be strange. Bill Gates to Elon Musk works.

It helps massively if the person making the ask – the solicitor – is also giving at the level they are asking the prospect to contribute, whether it's millionaire to millionaire or modest monthly giver to modest monthly giver. We have assumed that you, dear reader, are not the ideal of the high net worth donor with a close-to-hand peer, but rather the under-paid and probably under-valued fundraiser working to change the world through major gifts. This book is for you. We can still help you to make the ask to high-value prospects – individuals, business leaders, foundation directors. And the 20 powerful tools will help you achieve a successful solicitation – every time.

No matter where you fit into the donor firmament, *part* of your credibility in this situation is built on *you* being a donor to your cause. When you yourself are a donor, you gain the moral right to ask anyone else for a gift. This is one of the reasons we ask all the professional fundraisers and board members we train or carry out consulting for to become donors to their cause.

Of course, you may not be making that ask alone, but working as part of a team. As well as using the tools to upskill yourself, you can also use them to coach others – a more junior colleague keen to learn, an impressive but uncertain CEO, a nervous board member or even a passionate volunteer attending a gala where they have to solicit donations from fellow diners.

Sorting our metaphors

Although the 5Ps model we've developed – Passion, Proposal, Preparation, Persuasion and Persistence – is systematic, it's not simplistic or mechanistic. People and their interactions are by their nature messy, which means any model has to allow for that messiness. The 20 tools offer you a flexible and powerful approach that take you through five stages in sequence. You'll notice we are basing the model on two linked metaphors, described below.

It's a set of cogs...

We represent the model as a set of linked cogs (Figure 0.1). The cogs metaphor illustrates three important ideas:

- The elements are interrelated and interdependent – none is effective by itself: making the ask is a process.

- A small movement in one cog can result in a significant movement elsewhere – to succeed, you need to work on noticing these changes using your acuity.

- Cogs can go backwards as well as forwards – if you get stuck you can go back and look again at an earlier stage or try a different tool, working on your flexibility.

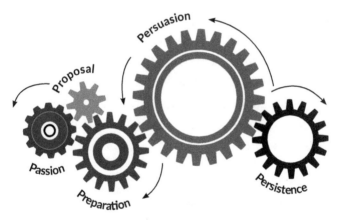

Figure 0.1: The 5Ps model

Please don't get carried away with the cogs metaphor. This is not meant to imply that if you do X you'll automatically get Y as a result.

Each chapter takes you through one of the interlocking 5Ps, outlining the purpose of each stage along with the skills and abilities you'll need to develop. The quick-start guide below tells you where in the book you can find the answer to specific challenges, and suggests the best tools to deal with them. For example, how to decide exactly what outcome you want from a situation, how to build rapport with 'difficult' people, how to handle a 'no' and how to recover from a setback.

... And it's a toolbox

One final bit of advice on the idea of a toolbox: you don't use all the tools in your box for every job. Each is there to do a specific task, or to offer you the choice that fits best with your particular challenge. Part of the skill in successfully making the ask is to choose the right tool for the job in hand and for the prospect in question. In some circumstances, you may need to spend longer working on what we call *hygiene factors* – issues that put a prospect off – rather than *motivators* – things that turn them on. At another time, the big issue might be deciding which of the four key ways you should present your case for support. Choose your tool or tools with care.

A story about toolboxes

Many years ago, Bernard was very excited to get a toolbox for Christmas. On Boxing Day, he opened up the box and looked for 'stuff to fix'. Years of bodged DIY in the house meant there were a number of nails that needed banging in. That looked easy. There were several kinds of hammer and it took some minutes to suss out what they were all for. (The amateur artisan, by the way, still doesn't know what the round-headed hammer is for.) But basically hammers were easy to use. And the results were good.

This was a very high-end toolbox. In it was a proper carpenter's plane for shaving wood. It too looked easy to use. And seemed ideal to fix the outside door that got stuck when it rained. But 20 minutes later it became apparent that a plane really requires skill. Otherwise, you get BIG chunks of wood coming off the door. That summer it became apparent that the amateur artisan had taken off way too much wood and there was a wide gap when the wood was dry. It turned out that the door needed to be properly painted to be waterproof and to stop the swelling. The careless carpenter had misdiagnosed the challenge and as a result used the wrong tool.

Moral: some tools are easy, and some require practice and skill. Make sure you've properly thought through your challenge and choose your tool with care.

Your Making the Ask toolbox

Below is a quick summary of the tools you have available – four in each stage. First think about the stage you're at and then choose the tool that matches the current challenge you want to tackle. Based on our experience, we've added a note on how much effort you need to put into becoming good at using them. The practice grade (Table 0.1) runs from 1 = super easy to 5 = pretty hard. Give yourself a break and begin with some of the easy ones.

Table 0.1: Practice grade

1. Passion	1. Create a powerful emotional anchor Use this when you're not feeling confident about your ability and need a boost. Practice grade: 3 Flick now to p. 6.	2. Establish your personal brand Use this when you need to change a prospect's perception of you and/ or your organisation. Practice grade: 2 Flick now to p. 14.	3. Create a philanthropic PIN code Use this when you want to share your key 'convincers' – hygiene factors and motivators – in the right sequence. Practice grade: 3 Flick now to p. 20.	4. DOSE the prospect: become a donor drug dealer! Use this when you want to engage your prospect at a deep neurological level. Practice grade: 5 Flick now to p. 33.
2. Proposal	5. Build an =mc story arc Use this when you're looking for the strongest way to shape and share your case for support. Practice grade: 4 Flick now to p. 46.	6. Hold out for a hero Use this when you need one of three powerful character options to put at the centre of your case for support story arc. Practice grade: 4 Flick now to p. 56.	7. Price your philanthropic propositions Use this when you want to match the prospect's potential to give with their particular passions. Practice grade: 2 Flick now to p. 62.	8. Check for (sticky) SUCCESS Use this when you need to ensure your messages are impactful and memorable. Practice grade: 2 Flick now to p. 74.
3. Preparation	9. Develop a well-formed outcome Use this when you want to establish in your mind the clear goal you wish to achieve	10. Set out your LIM-its Use this when there are a range of concrete outcomes available – some you'd	11. Flexibly reframe Use this when you may need to radically change the way your idea is received or perceived by	12. Link think, feel, do Use this when you want to directly connect what the prospect knows, how they feel and

	at the end. Practice grade: 4 Flick now to p. 96.	Like to, some you Intend to and some you Must achieve. Practice grade: 2 Flick now to p. 108.	your prospect. Practice grade: 3 Flick now to p. 114.	the action you want them to take. Practice grade: 3 Flick now to p. 131.
4. Persuasion	13. Try philanthropic pre-suasion – prime for success Use this when you think you can create a context that will make your approach more attractive before you even start to Ask. Practice grade: 3 Flick now to p. 141.	14. Pay absolute attention with the silent listen Use this when you need to be super focused on what the prospect has to say – and stop thinking about what you want to say. Practice grade: 3 Flick now to p. 149.	15. Build rapid rapport Use this when you have to engage with a prospect who is very different from you – and you need to look for social and psychological similarity. Practice grade: 4 Flick now to p. 158.	16. Match language style – switch sensory systems Use this when you discover the prospect has a different way of talking and thinking about the world. Practice grade: 5 Flick now to p. 172.
5. Persistence	17. Pivot perceptual positions – choose another angle Use this when you need to gain a different perspective on how your ask is going or want to review how it went.	18. Anticipate killer questions Use this when you know your organisation has some weaknesses or challenges and you need to prepare your response.	19. Call your mental mentors – ask for help Use this when you are really stuck on next moves and need some super expert advice to help you succeed.	20. Manage the nine fundraising 'no's Use this when you hear a 'no' to your proposition but want to establish whether there is an alternative possible approach.

	Practice grade: 2	Practice grade: 1	Practice grade: 3	Practice grade: 1
	Flick now to p. 189.	Flick now to p. 204.	Flick now to p. 208.	Flick now to p. 213.

1. Passion

2. Proposal

3. Preparation

4. Persuasion

5. Persistence

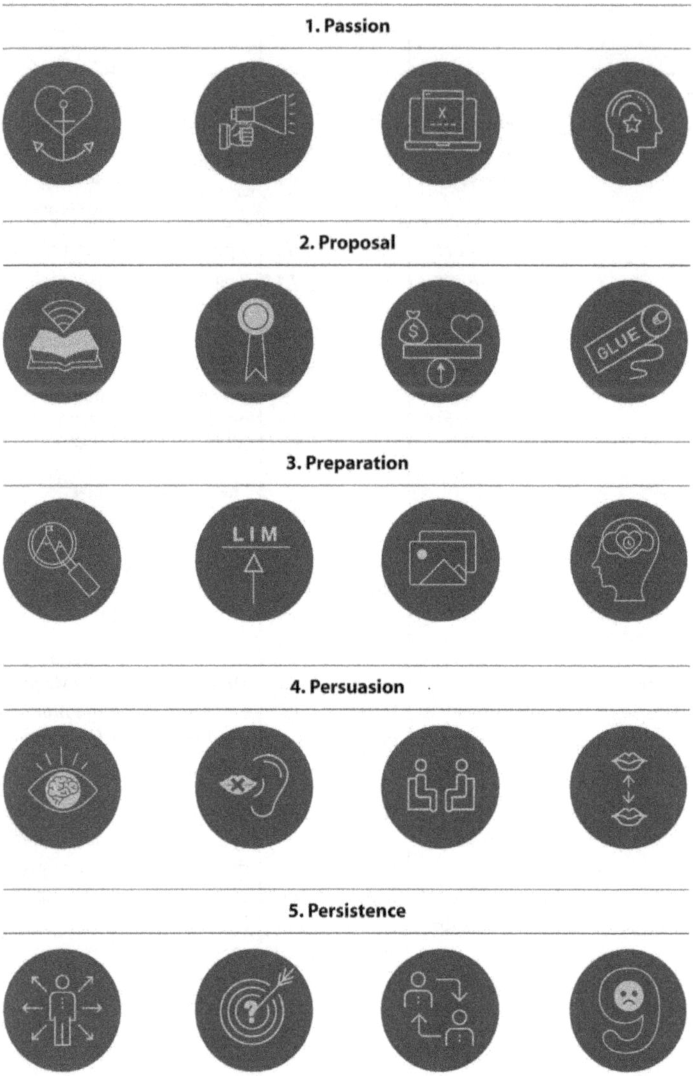

Figure 0.2: Making the ask toolbox

A final word on the ethics of making the ask

We need to talk about ethics before you dive into the toolbox.[2]

The tools and insights from psychology, neuroscience and behavioural science we lay out in these chapters are powerful – put simply, they work. That power means it's important to devote some space to discussing the ethics involved in using them. The question we have always asked ourselves when sharing them with our clients is: just because we *can* learn how to 'nudge' prospects to give more, *should* we use this knowledge?

First, let's put the question into context. Anyone engaged in fundraising should be aware of and adhere to relevant professional standards. Here in the UK, where we are based, we legally need to ensure that our work meets the Fundraising Regulator's *Code of Fundraising Practice*. Any members of the Chartered Institute of Fundraising or the US Association of Fundraising Professionals also commit to upholding certain professional and ethical standards. Those standards commit you to not using undue pressure with a prospect and to being open, honest and transparent. Anyone reading this book should read and be committed to these or a similar set of standards. The question then becomes whether the tools and nudges themselves violate these standards.

---

[2] We are indebted in this section to the work of the thoughtful Meredith Niles, Executive Director of Fundraising and Engagement at Curie Cancer Care in the UK, from whom we have quoted extensively. We have worked with her on several projects – including another book, *Change for Better* (2021), which looks at the broader implications of behavioural science for fundraising.

We'd argue that there is nothing inherently unethical in the use of the 20 tools we share here, *provided* they don't undermine the autonomy or the welfare of the prospect. Note the two key words there – *autonomy* and *welfare*. We borrow these from the work of Cass Sunstein, in his wonderful book *The Ethics of Influence*.[3] Although Sunstein was writing specifically about the ethics of government applying nudges to influence its citizenry, much of his framework can be applied to fundraising and to *Making the Ask*.

Autonomy

Autonomy is violated if we take away the prospect's ability to make a free choice. Our first question is: do any of the tools or underpinning insights in this book undermine a prospect's free choice? We don't see how they do. Yes, you have an obligation to tell the truth, but that doesn't mean you can't present your truth in the most compelling and attractive way. If you know that prospects are more likely to respond when you show them that other people have made a similar decision, why not offer this information? Provided everything you say is true, you haven't undermined their ability to make a free choice.

Welfare

Does using any of these tool insights undermine a prospect's welfare? There are safeguards in place within the framework of existing legal and professional standards to ensure that a prospect's giving doesn't harm them. These

---

[3] Cass Sunstein, *The Ethics of Influence* (2016).

include protections for vulnerable people who cannot exercise free choice. The codes described above require fundraisers to consider whether taking a donation would leave a prospect in financial hardship. It's also worth saying here that embedded in the question about damaging prospect welfare is the assumption that a gift to charity must necessarily correspond with a decrease in prospect welfare. This is a flawed interpretation of how prospects and donors relate to charities. We aren't playing a zero-sum game with charitable income on one side and donor welfare on the other. If nothing else, there is a significant body of evidence demonstrating that, when they are affordable and freely made, gifts to charity *increase* donor wellbeing. They do this by making donors feel good about themselves, by giving them a sense of agency when confronted with complex problems, and more. The DOSE chemicals we outline in Tool 4 are actually good for you!

Provided you are operating within the relevant professional and ethical standards, it's hard to see how using our toolbox could compromise the welfare of your prospect or donor.

But 'do no evil' is not enough: fundraisers should go further. We believe fundraisers have a positive obligation to make communications as effective as possible. Your beneficiaries need you to deliver results, and your prospects should be able to trust you to make the best possible use of the money they give you. It costs the same amount of money to mail an effective fundraising letter as it does to send a poor one. If you waste an hour on a poorly structured but heartfelt conversation with a major prospect using some inefficient approaches, you haven't done an ethical job. You've just done a poor one and wasted your time and the time of your prospect. More worryingly, you've lost an opportunity to build the refuge, to feed hungry children, to create the university access programme, to make the theatre accessible to all, to buy the gifted musician the violin their talent deserves. Prospects *expect* you to do the best job you can to secure their support. And now that you know there is a massive body of peer-reviewed, serious, scientific research, conducted at scale by very clever people – including several Nobel laureates – then tested by us across cultures and challenges that can help you make your fundraising ask more effective, isn't it professionally and morally negligent *not* to try to take advantage of it?

We're not saying ethics is simple or easy. Trust and confidence are so important to charities that it's always worthwhile pausing to take stock and reflect on whether an action is ethical as well as effective. Some of the world's best and most ethical charities are using the ideas in this book to achieve amazing results. Join the club!

Chapter 1

Passion

Nothing great in the world has ever been accomplished without passion.

Friedrich Hegel

One of the things we've learned from behavioural science is that emotion, and not reason, is the most powerful driver of human behaviour. We're going to call the level of emotion needed to fundraise successfully from HNWI *Passion*.

The starting point for introducing passion into your ask is to convince *yourself* that this work you are raising money for is genuinely important and you can be successful. *You* must have passion for your idea, cause or proposition. To be clear, we're not asking you to be a crazed zealot who believes nothing else in the world is important. But you do need to show that you care deeply. You also need to be able to generate, if not passion, then a positive and open approach in the mind of your prospect. The four tools we explore for passion are:

1. How to create the ideal state for yourself so you're inspired using an *emotional anchor.*

2. How to manage your personal brand to make a suitable impact using the ABC of *personal brand.*

3. How to create a receptive state in prospects by identifying their *hygiene factors and motivators* to discover their *philanthropic PIN code.*

4. How to create the key chemical connections using *DOSE.*

Figure 1.1: The passion power tools

How can you inspire yourself?

You have almost certainly heard of Pavlov and his famous dogs. The legendary Russian scientist won the Nobel Prize for Medicine in the early twentieth century for his studies in psychology, including his work with animals. He was especially interested in the extent to which many human and animal instincts are conditioned – that is, developed over time to be an automatic habit.

In his most famous – and cruel – experiment, he caged a number of dogs in a room and did not feed them until they were ravenous. He then brought cooked meat into the room. As you can imagine, when the dogs smelt the meat they immediately began to salivate – part of an autonomic response connected to releasing digestive juices. This strong response to food smells, of course, is common in all mammals including humans. In the experiment, as the smell wafted into their cage, Pavlov or one of his assistants added something else to the sensory mix for the dogs, specifically to generate an association. They rang a school hand bell to create a connection – a conditioned response – between the bell and the smell. (They later tried a metronome… it wasn't just bells that had the effect.)

Pavlov and his team repeated this experiment a number of times with the same dogs – on each occasion starving them, bringing in the delicious-smelling meat and ringing the bell. The team also ran the experiment over several months with different groups of dogs. After repeating the cooked meat + bell sequence around seven times with any group of dogs, Pavlov found that simply ringing the bell caused the animals to salivate. By this point, the stimulus of the bell ringing was so strongly associated in the dogs' minds with the smell of the meat that they were conditioned to automatically salivate at the sound of the bell alone. Pavlov had identified what we now know to be an emotional anchor – a stimulus that produces a specific, unconsciously created response.

This is not only a psychological effect but, as we now know, a neurological one – the dogs' brains had literally created new synaptic connections that the stimulus 'fired'. Given the right stimulus, the same neurological 'rewiring' also happens in humans. You can experience this phenomenon when a certain smell perhaps reminds you of your child-hood – maybe a comfort food or your mother's perfume. A song on the radio may lift your mood or reduce you to tears as a memory is invoked. Not all anchors are good. We drink or smoke too much without thinking when we're sad. And addictions or phobias are often learned unconsciously in the same way and are tough to 'unwire'.

Note that we're going to use the word 'anchor' later in the book in a slightly different way, but for the moment the key definition is 'a stimulus that promotes an automatic, unconscious response in the recipient'.

So why is this animal experiment from almost a hundred years ago relevant to you and to the process of seeking financial support? Well, we can create positive anchors for ourselves. Used properly, these can trigger a powerful and useful emotional response in you as and when you need it – physiologically and psychologically. Think of it as like having a special magical power you can turn on at will, rather like Ironman suiting up. Whether you're getting ready for a meeting, dialling a call, standing up for a presentation or even typing an email, being able to access the most appropriate anchor will provide you with whatever emotional state you need – confident, attractive, smart and so on.

It's especially useful to call on this 'mental superpower' if you just don't feel in the right place emotionally for that vital interaction with the prospective donor. For example, you get up bright and early to go to a vital prospect meeting. You come downstairs to eat breakfast and…

- Your phone beeps – the latest credit card statement has arrived, and you see you forgot to pay the last bill (when you had the cash) and a whopping amount of interest has been added.

- You're so distracted by this financial failure that you burn your toast and allow your tea to stew beyond drinkability. Breakfast is a washout.

- You set out to the station to catch the train into London without checking the forecast and without an umbrella. It begins to rain five minutes into your 20-minute brisk walk.

- It gets worse. En route you step in some dog poo, which proves impossible to wipe off your shoe on the grass nearby.

- As you step over to the kerb to try to scrape your poo-ed shoe on the edge, a passing car drives through a puddle and splashes you.

- You get on the train and have to stand all the way to your stop – aware that you smell of dog poo.

You're not having a great day and your spirits and confidence sink. Worse still, you find yourself almost looking for someone to vent your frustration on. None of this is a good mindset from which to seek financial support from a philanthropic prospect. What you need is an anchor to get you back into a resourceful – powerful – emotional state. Let's try that.

Tool 1:
Create a powerful emotional anchor

When to use it: When you're feeling low energy or unconfident in yourself or your cause.

Practice grade: 3

We've identified six steps to set up an anchor for yourself – fortunately none as dramatic or as cruel as the Pavlovian example. Essentially what you need to do is to train yourself to access a more positive mindset and emotional state using a quick and easy self-administered stimulus. Creating this positive and empowering mindset involves creating an emotional anchor. Anchoring is simple in itself, but it isn't easy to start with. It's a technique you need to practise – hence the grade 3 ranking.

Think of an anchored state as the equivalent of you loading up new and better software to replace the inappropriate version you've been using.

Six steps to creating a resourceful anchored state

Ideally, you should practise these steps in a quiet place, free from other distractions.

- *Step 1: Begin with the end.* Ask yourself how you'd like to feel (your state) when you're anchored. Be as specific as you can – the more concrete you can be the better. 'Feeling cheerful' may be too vague and you'll find it harder to get the result you want. Try something more specific, like 'Feeling enthusiastic and able to energise others.' This example might be suitable if you want to motivate the fundraising volunteers at a make-or-break campaign meeting.

- *Step 2: Decide on the anchor.* What's the specific stimulus you're going to use to anchor your state? While many stimuli can be used as an anchor – a sound, a smell, etc. – the easiest is usually something you can access without any external stimulus. The ideal approach is a physical trigger you give yourself – for example, squeezing an earlobe or pressing your fingers together in a particular pattern. Note that the stimulus needs to be different from anything you'd normally do. If it's too 'everyday' – such as scratching your nose – the danger is you'll either trigger it accidentally or ignore the stimulus altogether because it doesn't stand out for you. You'll need different anchors for different states. Be imaginative.

- *Step 3: Trigger a resourceful state.* Recall a real and relevant past experience of being in the emotional and psychological state you want to achieve – where you were successful and felt resourceful. It's very important that this is a real experience, but it needn't be exactly the same as the situation for which you're preparing. Staying with the example of a make-or-break fundraising campaign meeting, you might not have been in that situation before, but you could recall how you felt when you were able to convince a prospect to double their gift. Or even the time you were able to persuade that unhelpful hotel manager to upgrade your room when he didn't want to. Bring back the experience as vividly and intensely as you can. Be sure you are associated – that is, you're actually in that time, at that place, living that event from your own point of view. (For more on this, see how to switch perceptual positions in Chapter 5.) You may find it easier to close your eyes to do this. Switch on all your senses and listen to what's being said by you and others. Notice how you feel, see the expression on the other person's face.

- *Step 4: 'Fire' the anchor.* When you're fully associated in your resourceful experience, you'll reach a peak of intensity when it all seems quite vivid and real. At this point, apply the physical stimulus – or 'fire' the anchor you've chosen. Think of it like a Bluetooth connection between your brain and the physical sensation. You may have to do this for as much as a minute. Remember, you're trying to create a big change in your mental software and get those pesky neurons to rewire and fire together. (It sometimes takes a while for a Bluetooth connection to work.)

- *Step 5: 'Fix' the anchor.* It takes practice to ensure the anchor will create the state you want on demand, so be prepared to work at it. This is technically called 'fixing the anchor'. What you're doing is rewiring those neurons. To fix it, you need to learn to move quickly and easily between your peak and normal state. When you've completed Step 4, after a minute remove the physical anchor. At the same time, quickly reduce the mental and emotional intensity of the experience you're recreating – in your mind, soften the sound, turn any pictures in your head to black and white, and calm down the feeling. The purpose of this is to help you feel what it's like getting in and out of the state.

Repeat Steps 4 and 5 several times until you're confident the stimulus works and the state is the one you want. You should practise until you find it easy to get in and out of the resourceful state.

You may want to fire your anchor quickly and in awkward situations. If you've been practising with your eyes closed, do the same with your eyes open. Try firing your anchor on a bus or in a crowded place as well as in quiet rooms. When you can quickly and easily move from the unresourceful state to the resourceful one you want, you're equipped to use the technique 'live'.

- *Step 6: Use the state.* You're now ready to face your challenging situation. Practise the technique as often as you can. And remember that you may need different anchors for different situations – so once you've made the technique work in one way, try some different anchors (Table 1.1).

Table 1.1: Finding your anchor

Current state	Desired state	Anchor
Jumpy and nervous	Calm and confident	Pinch your earlobe
Bored and unengaged	Excited and passionate	Touch your chin with your thumb
Over-excited and too passionate	Rational and clinical	'Bite' your tongue
Tired and ready to give up	Energetic and ready to try again	Place your forefingers together

Sharing your 'inner glow' – your brand

Your inner state is important, and provides the starting point for getting you mentally ready for the ask. But you also need to create a powerful positive impression on the prospect. For that we need our next tool.

 Anchored athletes

Does anchoring sound a bit weird? Maybe it does in a conventional work sense, but this same technique is very common in sports psychology – especially in individual high-performance events. If you pay attention, you'll notice how many athletes do this. One of the most famous – seen repeatedly – is Usain Bolt's 'lightning' gesture. The smile and pointing with his hands are not random. He created the signature gesture with his coach to give himself an anchor for being 'the fastest man in the world' – as fast as lightning. The gesture is tied to the positive feeling he has of being confident and fast. In addition, we have a suspicion that he does it to make clear to the other athletes they are not as fast as him, thus creating a negative anchor for them.

You're probably also aware of the emotional impact Colin Kaepernick's brave 'taking the knee' gesture has had worldwide – so much so that many athletes from every discipline – and ethnicity – now do it. You can see the emotions it anchors in them, and often in us.

Impostor or deluded?

When you're mapping your personal brand, the trickiest part can be accurately assessing your own abilities by either wildly under-estimating them, called impostor syndrome, or wildly over-estimating them, the Dunning-Kruger effect.[1] Let's focus on imposter syndrome, which seems to be a more widespread and challenging issue – particularly, but not exclusively, for women.

---

[1] First detailed in 1999 by two researchers at Cornell University, David Dunning and Justin Kruger, this is a cognitive bias that encourages people to have a false sense of their own ability. The Dunning-Kruger effect has two elements:

(1) People mistakenly assess their ability as much higher than it really is, and think they are capable of things they're not. If you've ever watched the auditions for a singing talent show such as *X Factor* or *American Idol*, you can see plenty of evidence for this – and even more so on *The Apprentice*. It's a widespread phenomenon.

(2) Highly skilled people may *under-estimate* their relative competence, assuming activities that are easy for them will also be easy for others. This form of 'modesty' can, unfortunately, lead to over-expectations of colleagues. If you find many of the techniques described in this book easy, you may find it hard as a manager to understand why someone else finds them more challenging.

Impostor syndrome was first described by two US psychologists, Pauline Clance and Suzanne Imes, in a 1978 article.[2] They defined the phenomenon as 'an individual experience of self-perceived intellectual phoniness'. For their research, they interviewed 150 high-achieving, professionally recognised women. All the participants explained they didn't feel they 'owned' their success: they worried it was down to luck, or to others who over-estimated their ability or intelligence. Some saw it as a combination of the two. This self-doubt could cause serious career challenges: the women wouldn't apply for more senior jobs, or had wellbeing challenges with poor self-esteem, low self-confidence, anxiety or even depression.

In follow-up research, Clance and Imes identified that the syndrome was compounded by gender stereotypes, social norms or even the organisational culture in the person's workplace. Impostor phenomenon is believed to be less prevalent in men – but it does exist. It certainly affects many high-achieving fundraisers – as a glance at the agenda for any major conference will tell you. And it can be a crushing burden when getting ready to make that vital ask. If you recognise yourself or a colleague in this brief description, here's our simplest advice:

1. Acknowledge that this feeling is a normal response and that it is genuinely how you feel. Don't try to pretend it doesn't exist.

---

[2] Pauline Clance and Suzanne Imes, 'The impostor phenomenon in high achieving women: Dynamics and therapeutic intervention' in *Psychotherapy: Theory, Research & Practice*, 15(3), 241–247 (1978).

2. Confront your inner critic: write down your fears in one list and in another list the facts – the projects or activities where you are acknowledged to have succeeded.

3. Identify peers you respect and seek validation from them about your achievements. Don't be afraid to share your feelings – and maybe even encourage them to share theirs.

4. Create several emotional anchors based on positive mindsets that draw on feelings of success. Work hard to gain easy access to these anchors when the inner critic pops up.

Finally, you may also find the technique based on adopting perceptual positions discussed in Chapter 5 helpful here.

Tool 2:
Establish your
personal brand

When to use it: When you have to convey a specific impression or appearance – either because it would suit the prospect or to fit with your organisation's brand.

Practice grade: 2

It's great that you're in a strong internal mental and emotional state. You now need to consider the external perception of you by the prospect you're approaching. This is partly a function of who you 'normally' are. It's important to be authentic, but the impression you create should also align with how you need to come across in this specific professional setting and in line with your organisation's brand. For that reason, you may need to adjust your appearance and behaviour, and answer the question 'What is my personal brand?'

A personal brand is based around your ABC:

A = your attitude. What mindset or mental approach do you want to share?[3]

---

[3] This might be different from your anchor.

B = your beliefs. What are the values you hope to convey in the interaction?

C = your competencies. What is it you want to appear good at that will inspire confidence?

In each case, you need to be clear about the evidence you'll present to back up each element.

Consider Ashraf. She works for a prestigious university as a fundraiser. One department in the university is engaged in long-term basic research into an area that might have implications for identifying a cause of – and possible cure for – dementia. She approaches her prospect with the following ABC.

Table 1.2: Sample ABC for Ashraf

Element	Evidence – external behaviours I need to display to match this element
Attitude	I should be serious and considered. This is a very important and challenging subject and one about which we need to be transparent and honest. Much basic research in science and medicine finishes at a dead end. ('So now we know that's not the answer.') This caution is, in one sense, a good thing for science and the scientific method, but in my pitch I need to express pragmatic positivity for what the supporter's gift might achieve. I mustn't 'oversell' the potential for a cure.
Beliefs	I should convey a high regard for the world of serious science and my colleagues. I may well need to focus on the importance of excellence and how the researchers are chosen for their brilliance from all over the world. And I need to show respect for my institution, with its long tradition and heritage as well as academic rigour.
	I also need to be aware that many donors to medical causes have a direct family connection to the issue being studied. Many are desperate to contribute to the search for a cure. I should respect that sensitivity. I should also do some initial research into the prospect's connection to the cause.

Competences	I'm not a scientist, but I should demonstrate a basic understanding of the various research strands being undertaken. I need to be able to explain them in layperson terms so the prospect can understand them.
	And I also need to be familiar with the tax implications of different forms of gift – a legacy, a major gift from a company, a major personal gift, a gift from a UK resident or a US resident.

Now consider Ashraf's sister, Norwan. Norwan works for an experimental theatre company, again as a fundraiser. Her ABC is different.

Table 1.3: Sample ABC for Norwan

Element	Evidence – external behaviours I need to display to match this element
Attitude	I might want to be a bit gung ho and convey the excitement of the company and its work. Experimental theatre is about taking risks, and I need to convey the idea that there's no guarantee of critical success in any production. In my pitch, I must express delight about what the supporter's gift might achieve for art, for this kind of theatre and for our company. I need to be and sound excited about our work.
Beliefs	I should convey enthusiasm and commitment to colleagues. I may need to be a bit more critical of the fact that most funding goes to 'conventional' theatre. And I must be well versed in arguments for the transformative value of experimental arts – not simply as value for money. (Although I need also to have done my homework, so I don't patronise a prospect who shares that view.)
	I understand that many donors to artistic causes do it for fun and excitement. I need to get across how exciting their support would be for them.
	The company is keen to be inclusive in terms of casting. I need to be able to explain the rationale for that if the prospect has a challenge.
Competences	I'm not a theatre artist, but I should demonstrate familiarity with the various elements that make up the production. I should be able to explain any distinct features of our working method – improvisation, verité, naturalism or whatever.
	And I need to be familiar with the tax implications of different forms of gift – a legacy, a major gift from a company, a major personal gift, a gift from a UK resident or a US resident.

Notice that in every case the ABC needs to take account of what you already know about the prospect from any previous contact or research. Whatever you do, don't patronise the prospect by over-explaining something they already know. But equally don't assume that they are as fully up to speed with ideas in your discipline.

 Top tip: Clothes maketh the man... and woman

Your appearance can make an extraordinary difference to the way you come across. Although we're reluctant to offer fashion advice, it *is* important to consider your choice of clothes. Some of this is practical. Will that jacket be too hot in a well-heated prospect home? If so, there's a danger you'll sweat. Will that skirt be too short if you sit on a chair that tilts back?

Also be aware that people do ascribe status to different dress codes.

In a famous Australian experiment, a young man jaywalked against the pedestrian lights at a traffic crossing in Sydney.

When he was dressed in shorts, a surfer t-shirt and flip-flops (thongs), the great majority of the other pedestrians at the crossing tut-tutted, looked askance and stayed on the pavement until the lights changed.

The same young man repeated the experiment 30 minutes later, with a broadly similar group of people at the crossing. The only difference was he had changed into a smart business suit and was carrying a briefcase.

This time when he crossed the road against the lights, around a third of the people at the crossing followed him.

A second example involves the world-famous violinist Joshua Bell. In a 2007 experiment he went busking to see if the public would recognise one of the finest talents in the classical world. He dressed casually, stuck a baseball cap on his head and began playing at a Metro station in Washington. Audiences would often pay $200 for a seat at his concerts, but of the 1097 people who passed by while he played exquisite Beethoven, hardly anyone stopped. In fact, only 27 gave him any money, and just seven actually stopped and listened for any length of time. In a final comment on the importance of dress, instead of his normal fee of $50,000 per concert, he made… $52.17.

The learning? Dress to impress… show you're worth it.

How can you inspire your prospect?

You're now inspired, and you have an appropriate and aligned brand. Next you need to think about how you can similarly inspire your prospect. This involves understanding something about how people are generally motivated – and demotivated.

For help here, we turn to psychologist Fred Herzberg. He based his thinking partly on Maslow's well-known hierarchy of needs, but also on his experiences in World War II with troops and prisoners of war, then after the war with groups of staff and managers in large corporations. Herzberg's work explored which factors demotivate people and which cause people to be motivated. Two key findings for us were, first, that the sources of motivation and the sources of demotivation are different and distinct and, second, that one is not a mirror image of the other.

Tool 3:
Create a philanthropic
PIN code

When to use it: When you're trying to establish the key motivators and potential demotivators for a prospect.

Practice grade: 3

Not everyone is motivated or demotivated by the same things. And it's important to stress that *you are not the target market*, so your own motivations may not be a good guide to what will have the biggest positive or negative impact on a prospect.

Let's spend a bit more time with Herzberg. He called his two sources of motivation and demotivation hygiene factors and motivators.

Hygiene factors are potentially negative elements in any situation that have to be addressed in order for people to feel comfortable or safe – or ready to be motivated. In a work setting, these can be things like having a contract of employment with guaranteed rights, having clear lines of communication between staff, having the tools required to do your job, and employment terms such as salary and holidays being fair and honoured. People aren't normally actively motivated by these. But if any are missing, they will be dissatisfied or demotivated. If they are present, people adopt a neutral perspective.

People are actively satisfied by motivators. In a work setting, these can include a positive and inclusive culture, a salary system that is transparent and rewards effort, a manager who supports and encourages you, a clear chance for promotion and the possibility of autonomy in your work. Herzberg's big discovery was that these motivational factors only kick in once the hygiene factors are satisfied (Figure 1.2).

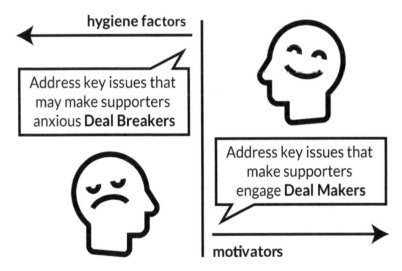

Figure 1.2: Hygiene factors and motivators

Looking at the diagram, the strong connection between Herzberg and the process of asking a prospect for support is immediately obvious. You need to begin by discovering as many of their motivators and demotivators as possible. You will base this partly on any research you do before the ask – maybe looking at previous philanthropy, or published sources if the person is a celebrity, or even what peers or friends of the prospect might tell you. It's worth creating two big lists of possibilities, then you can narrow them down using the philanthropic PIN code.

Hygiene factors in fundraising – especially for a major gift – are those elements that will help make the prospect feel secure. Without them, they may feel negative or anxious. Examples include:

- an up-to-date, well-structured strategic plan

- a clear governance structure with appropriate individuals in key positions

- a set of up-to-date financial accounts that show a positive/sustainable position[4]

- appropriate tax status – in the UK, charity registration; in the USA, 501(C)3 registration

- awareness of the tax implications of different kinds of donation or investment for the donor

- clear policies on things like the environment, anti-racism, equality of opportunity, diversity

- a track record of success in your field – and possibly even past awards or certifications of standards.

If any of these are not in place, the prospect may become anxious, unhappy or nervous. The presence of these factors is

---

[4] Of course, if the agency is in existential financial crisis, this needs to be made clear. Some supporters might be prepared to help you find your way out of the crisis, but it's always a bad move if they or their advisers *discover* a crisis.

not a motivator – no supporter has ever said, 'I've decided to make a donation as you have very clear and neat accounts...' It is the absence that causes the challenge.

Note also that there are some key interpersonal hygiene factors to consider. Is the prospect Ms or Mrs Jones, Robert or Sir Bob? If they're coming to visit you, do they eat peanuts? Drink wine? Eat bread? A small gaffe can get things off to a bad start. You need to do your homework *and* remain flexible. In the earliest part of the interaction – such as when you call to make an appointment or exchange emails – pay close attention to anything that might help identify a hygiene factor.

Motivators vary too, depending on the prospect, the agency for which you are seeking support and the specific proposition. They generally fall into some common clusters around:

- the opportunity for emotional or social rewards – maybe meeting a hero – and recognition

- a connection to deeply held values or beliefs, or to a sense of identity as a woman, as someone Scottish, as a gay man

- the chance to fulfil a dream or ambition – that of the prospect or someone significant to them

- a way to make a major contribution in a field or leave a personal legacy

- a means to honour someone the prospect loves or loved – a partner, parent or colleague.

You can use this broad framework to generate a bigger, more nuanced list. For a university, it might include:

- rewards and recognition – for example, an honorary degree, or naming a building

- access to senior staff – perhaps to meet award-winning scientists or academics[5]

- an appeal to contribute from – or a chance to meet – a respected figure or celebrity

- the chance to work with the senior team or board to contribute to strategy

- an emotional connection to a specific project – perhaps health related or childhood ambition

- an emotional connection to a specific institution – as an alumni

- the chance to make a major project happen that otherwise wouldn't

- a way to ensure specific groups – an ethnic or minority group, LGBTQI+ people, young women – are better represented.

---

[5] Our good friend Sue Fisher, formerly Director of Development at the Science Museum in London, and one of our fundraising heroines, tells of one major City dealer whose key ambition was to meet his hero, Stephen Hawking. After Sue arranged to seat him next to Professor Hawking at a dinner, the donor gave the museum a seven-figure gift – having previously delayed for five years.

For a theatre, it might include:

- recognition in printed programmes or even in the foyer, or on a seat or in a dressing room

- benefits such as access to performers – talking to actors, directors, even backstage staff

- a personal appeal over a private dinner from a respected artist or performer

- the chance to join the theatre's board and work with the senior team on future plans

- an emotional connection to a specific production – maybe where they met their partner

- the chance to make a project happen that otherwise wouldn't

- a unique, once-in-a-lifetime, behind-the-scenes opportunity to help make a production happen

- enabling excluded people – children, people with disabilities, elders – to enjoy theatre.

Remember, though:

- These motivators only kick in after the hygiene factors are satisfied.

- They are only motivators if the prospect feels they are – see the philanthropic PIN below.

CERN: Want to come and eat in the café?

We were delighted and proud to work on a small project with CERN in Switzerland, site of one of the world's largest and most extraordinary scientific experiments. Our goal was to help them raise funds for their educational work – engaging young people, especially young women, in science. The 'lab' is amazing, consisting of a huge tunnel under Switzerland and France where groundbreaking discoveries are taking place about the nature of fundamental particles. But the downside is that there's not much to 'see' because the results of the experiments consist mostly of streams and streams of computer data that take months of analysis. And even then, explaining high energy physics is... complicated.

So how can they motivate donors here? They have some simple and effective techniques:

- First, they allow you to ride around the giant underground complex on a bike – explaining as you do so that you're right next to some of the fastest moving particles in the universe. They dazzle you with some impressive facts and figures and some cool graphics.

- Then they take you to the staff café, where they ask you if you'd prefer to sit over there at the table with the scientist who won the Nobel prize two years ago... or at the table with some younger scientists who will probably win it in the next couple of years.

- If you are a really top donor, they may invite you to have dinner with someone really impressive. For example, you could meet Peter Higgs who won the Nobel Prize for identifying the Higgs Boson, the 'God particle'. (By the way, you're warned not to call it that when you meet him. He, and most other physicists, hate the phrase. Hygiene alert!)

You need to research the philanthropic history of your prospect where you can and where the General Data Protection Regulation (GDPR) laws allow. This can tell you a lot about their motivators. Read articles they have written. If they exist, watch YouTube videos of them speaking. The idea is to use this checklist to narrow down the motivators and identify those that are absolutely key. What we call their *personal philanthropic PIN*.

Be subtle in your conversation as you check out your thesis in conversation – people are not always candid about their real motivations. For example, not many donors would admit that their donation is because they want to look smarter than their peers and neighbours, although it's not an uncommon motivator. It's important to spend a bit of time trying to find out about the real underlying motivations. But whatever you do, don't 'call out' these small personal vanities. If you're keen to know more about the extent to which people dissemble about why they do what they do, read the brilliant and revealing *Everybody Lies* by Seth Stephens-Davidowitz.[6]

---

[6] Seth Stephens-Davidowitz, *Everybody Lies: Big Data, New Data, and What the Internet Can Tell Us About Who We Really Are* (2017).

We discuss another tool for uncovering motivations and decision-making processes in Chapter 4, called *acuity questions*. These are questions specifically designed to elicit candid, authentic answers without appearing to pry too much.

More than individuals

Hygiene factors and motivators are important for individuals, but we can also apply this tool to those who run foundations and corporations, which may be a source of substantial gifts. For example, in any kind of institutional setting, hygiene factors may include all those we've already listed, *plus* reputational risk. Often, the senior decision-makers in a company might be concerned with any potential for their investment to damage their brand or company. For a foundation, the question might be 'How closely does this proposal match our policy and objectives?'

There are some other very specific motivators in a corporate setting:

- the chance to improve or reposition their brand

- the opportunity to connect to a new customer or consumer base

- a channel to connect to customers' values – for example, Black Lives Matter

- a means to motivate employees by giving them the opportunity to volunteer[7]

---

[7] In our experience, this is proving to be increasingly important to companies.

- the chance to make business connections with other institutions or businesses

- a desire to signal a positive organisational culture

- specific interest from the board or senior leadership in the issue.

We explore good examples of matching commercial motivators in Chapter 3 with Tool 10: Set out your LIM-its.

Personal philanthropic PIN code

Your supporter's personal philanthropic PIN code is a unique combination of factors, which will encourage them to make a donation. As we've seen earlier, this small list derives from the bigger list you have generated under motivators. The idea of the personal philanthropic PIN is based on the four-digit numbers all bank account holders are given to access money from ATM machines. If you get the numbers and the sequence right, out comes the cash. If you don't, you fail. (Worse still, after three unsuccessful attempts you are locked out.)

In our experience, it's quite rare for someone to be motivated by one big single factor. They are much more likely to be driven by a combination of a small number of factors. The combination might include issues of gender and sexual identity, culture, background, beliefs or values, or past experience.

For example, this could be the philanthropic pin code for a woman keen to support a reproductive rights centre:

- my identity as a woman

- my sense of self as a feminist

- my position as a business leader in this town

- my desire to make sure young women like my daughters are safeguarded.

Whatever you do, don't make assumptions. In November 2020, it was interesting to hear US voters speaking about the presidential election. So many very conservative evangelical voters disliked much of what Trump said and did, but they voted for him because of his anti-abortion stand. And many Catholics felt torn about voting for Biden, himself a devout Catholic, because he supported the right to choose. People are complicated.

Here's another simpler example of a personal philanthropic PIN code for the CEO of a Glasgow-based SME making woven goods and being asked to support a heritage proposition in Scotland:

- their identity as a Scottish company – and keen to publicise that

- a desire to join with other leading Scottish companies 'to play in the big league'

- the opportunity for the CEO to appear with celebrities at heritage events

- a chance to associate their products with a traditional proposition.

Again, there's not always a clear linear connection between the 'obvious' PIN code and the real one. For example, when the Korean company Samsung first moved to the UK, many imagined they would support Asian festivals or even digital events. In fact, Samsung became a big donor to the Royal Shakespeare Company, a quintessential British brand, partly in a bid to reinforce their desired position as a proud 'UK' company.

Once you've built a hypothesis about your prospect's motivators, it's essential to check it out. We will give you more tools later to help you confirm it – or put it aside and research some more.

Motivation through admiration

Some years ago, we worked with the late, great Ruth Cardoso, respected academic and also wife of the former Brazilian president. We had been hired to help her fundraise worldwide for her highly respected foundation. We approached a well-known European grant-giving body to organise a meeting between the Brazilian board of trustees and the director of the body. We carefully explained to the grant-giver how the foundation's programme exactly matched their support criteria and how this would cement links between Europe and South America, help develop civil society in Brazil and meet the needs of poor Brazilians. The director gave us the unsmiling death stare of a man who was not impressed or interested. (Actually we think he didn't like one of us... wrong personal brand?)

We decided to try to build credibility by mentioning the individuals who were on the board of Dr Cardoso's foundation or who acted as advisers. We started with Dr Cardoso, herself a globally recognised academic and social anthropologist. The director's face remained stony. Then we mentioned perhaps the most famous Brazilian novelist – Paul Coelho. No reaction. The next name to drop was the Minister of Culture and musical icon Gilbero Gil. Nope, not a flicker of interest. Finally, we mentioned that on the board was the legendary Brazilian and global soccer genius Pele. The director smiled. "You mean *Pele* is associated with the foundation?" (As he said this, we noticed his foot kicked an imaginary ball under his desk and there was a complete change in expression.) "Yes," we said, glad to have got some reaction. "And I could meet Pele to discuss his involvement?" Us: "Yes, we guess so" (slightly puzzled). Suddenly things changed. We had discovered the grant-giving director's secret passion – football. And his hero was Pele. "Well," he said, "if someone of Pele's stature is involved…" For the chance to meet his hero, he would most definitely consider a proposal.

Tool 4:
DOSE the prospect –
become a donor drug dealer!

When to use it: As you choose your tool or approach the ask. Consider the neurochemical you're trying to stimulate in the prospect's brain.

Practice grade: 5

There is a family of four major chemicals that are important to anyone studying neuroscience because of the way they impact action. These chemicals are designed by evolution to work on different parts of our brain and body automatically and unconsciously to help us handle challenging situations. You've probably heard of these Four Horsemen of Amygdala: dopamine, oxytocin, serotonin and endorphins. The quartet can helpfully be remembered by the acronym DOSE. Together they are often described as the happy chemicals. Although their primary purpose is not actually to deliver happiness, if you're asking for support you should be trying to organise stimuli – words, images, experiences – in a way that promotes their production, and your cause.

1. *Dopamine* is the neurochemical responsible for motivation towards a goal or result. Importantly, it's about

the pleasure derived from anticipation rather than the actual result. And that anticipation is what drives us to keep trying. Levels of dopamine go up when someone is getting closer to a goal. For example, waiting at the airport to meet a friend or loved one could well stimulate high levels of dopamine in you – although meeting the person may in fact be less exciting than you imagined. A more prosaic example is repeatedly ordering pizza, which in your mind will be delicious – and then finding the first bite is, as usual, a little disappointing. Nonetheless people are addicted to dopamine and will repeat behaviour that delivers a measure, even if the long-term result is injurious. Just as in a drug addiction linked to dopamine, where the addict will give up eating, sex, relationships and so on for the next kick.

Implication: you need make sure your prospect is keen to achieve the goal you have set out. Maybe a diagram, or a graph showing how close the project is to success, will help here. Or giving regular updates on progress. Both approaches will help to stimulate dopamine.

2. *Oxytocin* is a neurochemical important in helping us operate effectively as social creatures. It helps build empathy and social bonding, and is even sometimes called the 'hug drug'. This is a drug on which we get hooked at a very young age. As a breastfeeding mother and her baby gaze at each other, oxytocin is delivered via her breastmilk. Experiments have shown that even when not feeding, subsequent eye contact between mother and child drives up oxytocin levels in both.

This bonding over eye contact is then wired in for life – for example, when lovers meet. For that reason, images that involve eye contact, especially where the subject has large pupils, promote a sense of empathy – driven by an increase in oxytocin. Not sure? Look at all the Disney characters and the size of the eyes of the hero/heroine. The purpose is to encourage you to feel empathetic towards the character.

Implication: you need to have a positive and empathetic relationship with your prospect. Look them in the eye when you speak to them. But you can be more sophisticated, too. If your ask is for a beneficiary cluster, then your words and images should focus on promoting oxytocin. For example, use pictures of individuals – perhaps children – looking up and out of your fundraising literature. Look especially for images where individuals have large eyes. You might also consider really working to help the prospect understand how it feels to be in that situation. This is not an easy proposition when it's an older man trying to understand what it's like to be a young girl trapped in poverty and having no access to menstrual products. (See also Tool 5: Build an =mc story arc in Chapter 2.)

3. *Serotonin* is another neurotransmitter. It acts as a regulator for mood and promotes a sense of self-worth and esteem. This is why a lack of serotonin is often associated with anxiety and depression. Serotonin plays an especially important role in hunger, since 90% of the body's serotonin is found in the gut microbiome. As a result, an imbalance and the associated

negative feelings can sometimes lead to binge eating. Serotonin makes us want to feel accepted and valued.

Implication: you can try to generate serotonin in an individual, perhaps by emphasising their importance in the community or portraying them as the business leader who will provide guidance and leadership to others. This kind of messaging is likely to produce a serotonin high. A key issue, of course, is to find out where the prospect gets their sense of esteem from. It might be that praise from someone they respect will more easily raise serotonin levels – a spouse, business partners, religious figures, celebrities, or even from their hero. See the Pele example earlier. And it's true that an ask after a good meal is more likely to generate a serotonin 'hit'. (Also have a look at Tool 6: Hold out for a hero in Chapter 2.)

4. *Endorphins* are what make you feel really good after a challenging run or a tough gym session – your 'high' is the result of a rush of endorphins. Their real purpose is to mask pain – which is what they're doing when you feel the post-effort high. This helpful drug is strongly connected to the fight or flight response vital to your evolutionary success – for finding food or battling an enemy. Endorphins occur naturally when we take exercise. You can measure particularly high levels of endorphins at the end of a charity run or charity walk.

Implication: even for a wealthy person, making a large gift can be quite emotionally if not physically painful. There may be a chance to acknowledge difficult explanations that will need to be made to other key stakeholders such as family. On a more practical level, persuading a prospect to take part in an activity with you can help to generate endorphins. The activity can be quite small, such as walking around your building, or much bigger, such as making a visit to a refugee camp. Explore the walk used by UDEM in Tool 13: Try philanthropic pre-suasion – prime for success in Chapter 4. Anything that involves a degree of physical movement can help to increase endorphins.

Together, these four chemicals can create a powerful impact on a prospect's receptivity to your message. A fabulous example is Scottish Opera, which persuaded a group of major donor prospects to pay for the installation of a lift. The purpose of the lift was to make it easier for elderly theatregoers or those with a disability to gain access to all parts of the building. Their tactic was to make an ask at the top of the building. To get there, the prospects had to walk up a lot of stairs, and as they did so, the fundraisers gave them their DOSE:

- *Dopamine:* the donors were being asked to provide the last chunk of cash that would ensure all the seats in the theatre would be accessible to older people or anyone with a disability. They anticipated success in the campaign, knowing they could make it happen as a group.

- *Oxytocin:* walking up all the stairs and experiencing the situation as it was for older people and those with a disability produced empathy. If the prospects had spent their lives going to the easy-to-get-to 'posh' seats in the stalls and dress circle, they were unlikely to have given this much thought previously.

- *Serotonin:* we imagine this was present in litres, with this small group of potential supporters feeling special and uniquely capable of making a difference. As a thank you, all the donors were given a piece of the old stair banister carved and with a plaque honouring their gift – Serotonin at Home!

- *Endorphins:* we think the physical exercise of climbing up a lot of stairs – and getting there somewhat out of puff – probably delivered a surge of endorphins. (Lots of the supporters were themselves slightly older and maybe a bit less fit.)

In summary, yes – we are saying your job is to be a donor drug dealer!

 Action summary

✓ Make sure you go to any interaction – meeting, email, Zoom call, phone call – having adjusted your mental and emotional state. You need to be in the right mindset to be successful. Developing one or more emotional anchors will help you with this.

✓ Next, ensure your personal brand is appropriate. What appearance and behaviour – clothes, language, manners, approach – would fit with your personal brand and with the brand of the organisation you're representing?

✓ Identify the hygiene factors and motivators in any given situation. Use a checklist. A prospect researcher can give you a clue to a prospect's likely motivators and hygiene factors, based on their philanthropic history. Begin by addressing the hygiene factors. Unless you have these in place, the motivators won't work.

✓ Don't assume that there is just one motivator or that what motivates you will also motivate the prospect. Identify the three to four key philanthropic PIN motivators you believe to be important for the prospect, and make sure to check these out when you're undertaking research or even during the conversation.

✓ Use the philanthropic PIN code to pinpoint the DOSE your prospect needs. How can you build their anticipation, make an emotional connection, build their self-esteem and offer them an achievement 'high'?

Chapter 2

Proposal

Everything should be as simple as it can be but no simpler.

Albert Einstein

Having followed all the advice and used a selection of the tools in Step 1 of the 5Ps model, you're now in the best possible mindset to move forward – and have done some thinking about what might be important to your prospect. But there's more to do before you consider direct communication with them.

We're calling this phase *Proposal*. It covers various ways of presenting your idea in a way that will appeal to your prospect and match their ability to contribute. To help you do this, we're going to share four useful and elegant tools:

- Create a compelling story or case for support using the =*mc story arc*.

- Choose the right *hero* to put at the centre of your story.

- Price a specific *proposition* within the case for support.

- Make sure your proposition is memorable by using the *SUCCESS formula*.

Figure 2.1: The proposal power tools

Make the case before making the ask

Apart from ubiquitous emails, fundraising communications can take a number of forms:

- a 200-character text message sent by WhatsApp to supporters' mobile phones calling for instant action to tackle a sudden crisis

- a Facebook ad that leads to a webpage encouraging a potentially interested party to click on a link and find out more about a cause

- a leaflet or brochure with an appropriate call to action that's picked up at an event and taken home by the prospect to read in their own time.

All these formats might ultimately lead to a meeting where a big ask is made. Most of them – along with other communications such as proposals, presentations and even speeches at events – will draw on a central structure commonly referred to as a *case for support*. It's this case that should be at the heart of your philanthropic ask.

A case for support explains to potential donors what you need money for and what the benefits will be. It is normally written by a campaign team or sometimes a specialist writer. Cases can be used in a range of fundraising settings, but they are viewed as essential in major gift, capital and endowment campaigns.[1]

A case is powerful and effective if it is:

- a clear, widely owned and understood vision of what is to be achieved

- a defined and costed list of the resources needed to achieve that vision

- aimed at a cluster of donors who have the potential to meet the expressed need.

When it is well constructed, your case serves a number of both internal and external uses. Internally, it:

- clarifies the need and its scale and urgency

- allows everyone from board members to volunteers to align around a specific set of messages

- forces you to simplify your messages

- provides a focus for fundraising energies.

Externally, it:

- forms the basis for communications with a wide range of stakeholders

- shares an easy-to-understand support message with prospects

---

[1] An endowment campaign is designed to create an investable capital sum that provides income for ongoing running costs.

- offers a range of options for anyone who wants to give support

- provides a core set of messages that can be translated into different formats and channels.

Sadly, many of the cases for support we see in the general fundraising literature use archaic or unsubstantiated formulas that have no specific evidential underpinning. Often these are just cookie-cutter approaches that appeal to the writer. In our experience of generating cases for a wide range of organisations, we've identified some key psychological principles drawn from behavioural science and other disciplines, which create powerful and flexible options.

The case should provide a substantial basis on which to communicate your need. It must be more than just a snappy mission statement or punchy strap line. But it also needs to be less than a lengthy philosophical enquiry into why your organisation should exist.

 The long and the short of it

Your case will end up existing in several forms – a longer version with detailed data and analysis backup, and a shorter, pithier one that encapsulates the central idea.

For example, we wrote a 30-page case for support document for a UK charity, the National Society for the Prevention of Cruelty to Children (NSPCC). It covered five sophisticated 'vision propositions' to ensure children were safeguarded and cared for in all situations. This work took several months – we did interviews, we ran focus groups with staff, users and other stakeholders, we ran an online survey. The result was a detailed, closely argued case backed by a robust budget. Then one day we had an urgent call from the campaign director. He had just learned that a key political networker and supporter was attending a reception being hosted by the British Prime Minister at 10 Downing Street at 6.30 that evening.

At 2.00 pm we met in a coffee bar and together we crafted a six-line version of the case for the networker to use with other guests. It had to be just as compelling as the 30-page version – and it was hard work.

In a sense, it was the classic elevator pitch – and a terrific exercise in the need to be able to strip your key message back to its core. (Oh, and it worked. And no, sadly we can't share it.)

Tool 5:
Build an =mc story arc

When to use it: When you need to have a simple way to present your case that allows you to key into the underlying decision frames of different people.

Practice grade: 4

A good case – in whatever form it takes – should tell a story. Not the kind you find in a novel or a movie, but rather a story arc – a mental journey on which you can take your prospect, potential supporter or social investor.

We've developed a case framework that we've now tested over a number of years. It fits some important behavioural science principles, assuming that people have a strong orientation along two dimensions (Figure 2.2):

- *time:* whether the outcome will happen now/soon or at some future point

- *impact:* whether the case will work towards a positive outcome or away from a negative outcome.

These dimensions relate to some central ideas in decision science.[2] The first involves a *tendency*, as a species, to prefer short-term benefits or payoffs. The second is a *tendency* or *bias* to avoid negative consequences or losses. But not everyone has these tendencies.

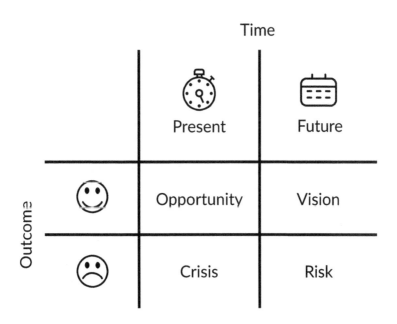

Time

Present   **Future**

Outcome

Opportunity   **Vision**

Crisis   **Risk**

Figure 2.2: Case framework

If you put these dimensions together in the possible combinations, you have four ways to present your story:

1. *A risk* – that is, a negative future. This is about sharing with the prospect a possible negative outcome that might happen if you and they don't take action. This message appeals strongly to people who:

   • prefer to avoid negative consequences

---

[2] If you want to know more you might try another book by Bernard Ross and Omar Mahmoud, *Change for Good*. See the booklist.

- tend to think in a longer-term way.

You're asking them to consider taking action to reduce or eliminate the possibility of this bad outcome happening in the future.

2. *A crisis* – that is, a negative present. This involves making it clear that an urgent and important situation exists that needs to be resolved. This message appeals strongly to people who:

   - prefer to avoid negative consequences

   - tend to think in a short-term way.

   You're asking them to consider taking action to reduce or eliminate the possibility of this bad outcome happening now.

3. *An opportunity* – that is, a positive present. This is about telling the prospect there is a short-term positive opportunity that could be taken advantage of. This message appeals strongly to people who:

   - prefer to opt for positive action

   - tend to think in a short-term way.

   You're asking them to seize the moment and take action to help make the good outcome happen – mitigating a negative or accelerating a positive.

4. *A vision* – that is, a positive potential future. This involves laying out a longer-term positive outcome that could be created. This message appeals strongly to people who:

   - want an active role in creating positive action

- tend to think in a longer-term way.

You're asking them to invest and take action to help make the possibility of this good outcome happening more likely.

You can use the matrix in two ways:

1. Identify the specific preference with which the prospect most strongly identifies – not everyone will respond the same way.

2. Share the story arc as a story narrative, beginning with risk and moving clockwise round to vision – allowing you to appeal to a wide range of preferences. Figure 2.3 illustrates this.

Opportunity

But with early positive action there is a possible opportunity

Vision

And with sustained action there could be wonderful vision

Tell your story in a journey form from negative possibility to future result

Crisis

The negative consequences could escalate to a crisis

Risk

If you don't take action there is a risk of negative consequences

Figure 2.3: Sharing the story arc as a narrative

We've illustrated each option using two different examples – the first a theatre education programme in a small town and the second an HIV/AIDS development agency in Africa.

Theatre example – focusing on specific preferences

Imagine the director of a local arts centre talking to a group of parents about the funding for the centre in response to a proposal from the council to cut the grant they receive for an education programme aimed at young people:

- *Risk:* 'If we don't secure the long-term funds for the education programme, within five years there will be a whole generation of young people denied access to the benefits of theatre workshops. A generation of young performers aged 10 to 15 will have lost the chance to learn expressive skills through the workshops we offer. *We need you to commit to a future for your children and grandchildren.*'

- *Crisis:* 'If we don't find funds for the education programme within the next three months, we'll have to close it down. Our skilled tutors will move away. The 300 young people who come to the workshops every week will lose faith in us. Our town and its 3,000 young people will have lost their only chance to take part in live theatre and gain the skills and confidence it brings. *We need you to step up and stop this happening now.*'

- *Opportunity:* 'Thanks to the shop closing, a large space next door has come free. Also, a major foundation is offering to match grants for initiatives supporting older adolescents at risk of going off the rails. If we raise the matching money in the next three months, we can acquire the space for the dedicated older teen drama studio we've been talking about for years. We can then offer drama workshops to the town's older adolescents – your sons and daughters – and in a few years bring in small visiting performances to create even richer learning. *We're hoping you'll grasp this opportunity. It's so close.*'

- *Vision:* 'The drama workshops are under the most threat from the cuts. We need to make sure they're not seen as a marginal subject by the council. And actually we want to give the young people *more*. If we can raise enough money, we could safeguard the workshops *and* organise a drama festival next year for the whole county – bringing together professional touring companies, local amateurs, youth theatres and more. It would really put the town, your kids and our work on the map. It could become an event of national importance and offer your daughters and sons a chance to shine. It'll also show the council we mean to be here for years to come. But festivals take a lot of time – and money – to organise. *We're hoping you share, and will join with us in, the excitement of what's possible.*'

HIV/AIDS example – going round the story arc

- *Risk:* 'Unless we create education programmes on condom use and ensure widespread anti-retroviral access to stem the growth of HIV transmission, in 10 years there will be two million children without parents – AIDS orphans – in Zimbabwe.'

- *Crisis:* 'At current rates of infection and with the current limited condom use and access to anti-retrovirals, 10,000 people in Zimbabwe will be infected and die needlessly in the next six months. Many of these will be parents, leaving children without adult carers.'

- *Opportunity:* 'We've secured a fantastic deal with a pharmaceutical company and a condom manufacturer offering 25% off supplies up to the end of the financial year. If we can fund the condom distribution programme in the next six months and secure access to anti-retrovirals, we can reduce infection by 60% by Christmas and save 10,000 adult lives in the next six months – and ensure their children are looked after in their own families.'

- *Vision:* 'By building a network of health centres and equipping them, we can ensure that within the next five years every person in Zimbabwe will have effective HIV treatment, whether it's protection through condoms or access to life-saving antivirals. We'll be offering people – and especially parents of young children – the chance to live full and productive lives.'

Which one works best?

It's interesting to consider which is the most powerful quadrant overall in fundraising. Take a second to reflect on which you believe normally works best.

We've asked that question in over 100 conference sessions in places as far apart as Brazil and India, Australia and Sweden. Almost universally, experienced fundraisers know the answer. The majority would like it to be 'vision' (positive future), but in practice – and from their experience – they know 'crisis' (negative present) is normally the strongest. The underlying psychology for this can be traced partly back to Maslow, whose hierarchy of needs is based around unmet needs. It's always worth your while to have an option to frame your case as a crisis – and useful, if you can, to have your case expressed in all four forms to allow for maximum flexibility.

Some points to consider:

- The behavioural science about our responses to loss and time applies generally. By implication, negative outcomes have a much more powerful impact on decisions than positive outcomes, which is why the idea of loss – actual or possible – underpins so many big fundraising campaigns. Think about the 2004 Asian tsunami, Australian bushfires, Syrian refugees…

- Crisis is generally the most powerful driver of decisions – hence the expression 'never waste a good crisis'. Having said that, individuals are not always predictable, and some may have a preference for another – or more than one – of the case option framings. Some *are* very attracted towards vision; others find opportunities really engaging; still others are drawn towards minimising risk.

- The elegant story arc in the HIV/AIDS example makes movement from risk to potential crisis to possible opportunity to future vision seem logical. In our experience, this is the most effective way to use the tool. It can be particularly helpful if you're trying to create a generalised message that both lets you tell the whole story and allows prospects to focus on the part that's important and interesting to them.

- Most cases will appear to you to fall quite naturally into one of the quadrants, and it's tempting just to use that one. Be careful, though, that you are not simply reflecting your own bias or preference. It's worth getting colleagues to work on other versions of the case to test out whether there genuinely is a natural affinity with the case itself in your version, or it's just *your* choice. In any event, you will need to practise being just as convincing and compelling when sharing the case in the other options.

Top tip: Talking or writing?

Telling a story person to person is definitely best approach from an impact and engagement point of view. You can immediately see the effect your message does or doesn't have, and adjust the content or approach accordingly during the telling. (See Tools 13 to 16 in Chapter 4 to help you do this.)

But sometimes you need to write the story down – in an email, on a webpage, in a proposal, a publication or even a brochure (called a 'leave behind'). Unfortunately, when stories are written down in detail, what they gain in structure and coherence they often lose in energy and authenticity because people tend to style switch into a more formal or convoluted English.

Our advice is to strike a balance. By all means have your prepared document and be ready to leave it with the prospect or send it to them. But also be ready and willing to share your brief version of the case 'live'.

Check to make sure your case has impact using the *SUCCESS* tool below. And if you need some advice on how to find out about someone's preference upfront, consider using *Acuity Questions* – part of Tool 14: Pay absolute attention with the silent listen.

Tool 6:
Hold out for a hero

When to use it: Your case is a kind of story, and stories need to have an identifiable hero or heroine. Use the hero approach to decide who's the key protagonist – with whom do you want the prospect to identify?

Practice grade: 4

Once you have your story structure, you need to decide who is the key protagonist – called the hero or heroine. (From now on we'll use 'hero' to signify either gender.) The purpose of the hero is to find a way for the reader or listener to identify more closely with the situation, and so feel a greater sense of agency or empathy.

There are three possible options for the hero of a fundraising story:

- *The organisation.* This could be the agency itself, but probably better the people who work for it – research scientists, campaigners, humanitarian activists, doctors, the artistic director.

- *The beneficiary.* This is whoever is in need – the refugee, the person impacted by an illness, the child in need of protection, the caregiver, the young artist needing a bursary.

- *The supporter.* This is whoever the message is targeted at – a volunteer, a social investor, a donor, a member and others who add value to your cause.

You need to decide which individual within your chosen category is the hero of the story. Ideally, it should appear to be someone real – Abdul, Jane, Sean or Eman. We say 'appear' because sometimes you should create a composite person to protect an individual's identity or offer anonymity. This is often the case when you're telling the story of a beneficiary – for example, a human rights activist who could be put in danger if identified. If you're using someone from the organisation, your hero can represent a more general cluster – for example, 'Dr Susan Jones the research scientist working to develop the cure for multiple sclerosis' could represent the many individuals and teams working on a cure. Sometimes it's best to choose someone who is typical rather than the 'leader' or most important figure.

 Organisation as hero

It's quite hard to make an organisation an engaging hero. But if you do choose to do this, make sure you're clear about the brand personality. Commercial companies use this all the time. Walmart plays 'The Regular Guy' in brand terms. Nike is 'The Champion', focusing on high achievers. And Ben and Jerry is 'The Jester' for its playfulness with food.

You can apply the same thinking to non-profits. Greenpeace might, for example, be 'The Rebel', campaigning on behalf of the planet; Macmillan Cancer Support could be the 'Caring Companion' of someone with cancer. Figure 2.4 shows a table with some possible personalities. Use this for inspiration but devise your own.

Brand personalities

The Caregiver (e.g. Macmillan)	**The Counsellor** (e.g. Childline)	**The Defender** (e.g. Amnesty)
The Doctor (e.g. MSF)	**The Guardian** (e.g. NSPCC)	**The Magician** (e.g. Cirque du Soleil)
The Protector (e.g. UNICEF)	**The Rescuer** (e.g. Red Cross)	**The Jester** (e.g. Comic Relief)
The Helper (e.g. Samaritans)	**The Rebel** (e.g. Greenpeace)	**The Warrior** (e.g. RNLI)

Figure 2.4: Possible brand personalities

Which one works best?

Which of the three hero clusters – organisation, beneficiary, supporter – is best? Often the answer in contemporary fundraising is the prospect.[3] Consider choosing them as a hero or portraying someone with whom a supporter or potential supporter can identify – an older woman donor, a millennial fan, a businessperson who sees themselves as a leader. There is a real, powerful impact if the supporter can see themselves in the story as a hero.

A key element of the supporter as hero approach is to ensure that they feel agency – a sense of power or the ability to act and address the challenge, or an identifiable aspect of it. This is especially important with an HNWI prospect who wants to feel that their investment gives them significant agency. To illustrate this, think about the difference between these three statements from a human rights organisation:

- 'Help us tackle the injustice of Jane Jones' imprisonment.' (organisation as hero)

- 'Please help Jane Jones challenge the injustice of her imprisonment.' (beneficiary as hero)

- 'Here's how you can tackle injustice.' (supporter as hero)

Next you need to decide why this person is a hero – why are they admirable? If you choose the prospect, they need

---

[3] Although our focus here is on HNWI prospects, we'd argue that the hero idea is best captured in the word 'supporter' to encompass live prospects at all levels. Someone who simply visits your website and signs up to receive your newsletter is a kind of supporter. Your task is to find out how to engage them in a way that helps convert them into a donor.

to be admirable in their own eyes, and in the eyes of those they respect – friends, family, colleagues, peers and so on. By making them the hero, you succeed in giving them a story to feel good about.

This could be because of:

- what they achieved

- what they contributed

- the example they gave

- a challenge they helped someone overcome

- the way they did something.

One of our favourite fundraising gurus, Tom Ahearn, imagines the supporter telling their friend or family a story. This great advice moves the emphasis away from you telling *your* story to helping the prospect tell *theirs*. (By the way, this is a terrific way to DOSE your prospects with the oxytocin for empathy and serotonin for esteem we discussed in Tool 4: DOSE the prospect: Become a donor drug dealer!) Here are some opening lines to stories that prospects might want to tell:

'I helped a child enjoy Shakespeare for the first time by supporting the theatre company to offer free seats.'

'I ensured that ancient woodland would be there in another 100 years by meeting the cost of the planting.'

'I guaranteed that no child at school had to try to learn while hungry by supporting the school breakfast club.'

If you do use someone else as the hero, check they are someone the target audience could connect with and build a bridge to. This is especially important if the hero is from a different country or culture, or has had an experience – an illness, for example – that others might not understand. If the hero is very different – which is often the case with a beneficiary – you need to think about how you can create empathy. Are you making the case and connecting to them as a mother, as a teacher, as someone who had a tough upbringing, as someone who loves reading, as a person of faith?

 'I saved a whole species for the next generation'

Before the former president of the Diane Fossey Gorilla Fund, Clare Richardson, met with Ted Turner to ask for the million dollar gift, we helped her to prepare a line to share with him: 'With your million dollar donation you will save an entire species [the mountain gorillas in Rwanda] for the next generation.'

We designed this phrasing so Ted could then say, 'I saved a whole species for the next generation' to his friends and associates. We think you'll agree it's much more powerful than, 'I gave a million dollars so someone else could save the species.'

Tool 7:
Price your philanthropic propositions

When to use it: This tool involves breaking down your overall case for support into specific propositions. Propositions are ways to combine your prospect's interest and their ability to give – linking money and motivation.

Practice grade: 2

It's quite rare for an individual donor or prospect to have the ability to meet the entirety of your need, although of course there are exceptions. On the other hand, some prospects want to meet the whole cost of a project in order to 'own' it. You need to decide whether such a gift is acceptable, ethical and sustainable, all of which may be reasons why you would choose not to be entirely dependent on one donor. For example, in the event of the scandal or a falling out, it can leave you or the organisation very vulnerable. (See the Vilar case study in Tool 18: Anticipate killer questions in Chapter 5.)

The basic challenge is that you may need to prepare for a meeting with a prospect or draft a proposition for them without being sure about their ability to give. (Although you could have an idea of a range.) Even with the best prospect research in the world, it is quite hard to have an entirely accurate idea of what another person's financial ability might be. Obviously past philanthropic history is a guide – but only a guide. Make sure you don't get trapped in a mindset where you go for the 'average' gift based on previous philanthropic history simply because it's the safest. You might miss out on an exceptional opportunity.

 Top tip: Giving by the numbers

We'll discover later on in Tool 11: Flexibly reframe in Chapter 3 that specific numbers can have an interesting effect on giving behaviours that doesn't relate to the ability to give. Here are some examples to whet your interest:

- Oxford University received a gift from an Asian donor of £8,888,888.80. The University didn't originally ask for that exact sum – what costs a weird sum like that? What's the explanation? The answer lies in the power of the lucky number 8 in some Asian cultures. (8 is the luckiest number in Chinese culture because 八 sounds like 發 (fa), which means 'wealth', 'fortune', and 'prosper' in Chinese.) The donor wanted to get some good fortune by writing a cheque for 8x8. Illogical? Yes. Worth working out a proposition that you could cost at that amount? Certainly!

- In the UK, pensioners and those over 60 receive a non-means tested – that is, universal – benefit of £200 to £300 a year to help with the cost of winter fuel. Because it's not means tested, many relatively wealthy individuals who don't need it receive the benefit. Canny charities will often send out propositions linked to this sum to this target market, asking them to make a gift, often connecting it to older people who *do* need the support. Receiving such a donation at this time is a clue that you have someone who cares about social issues and who doesn't need help to pay for fuel. A high-value prospect in the making?

- Harvard University is the world's richest university, with an endowment of $41.9 billion. Some would argue that it doesn't need more money. But Harvard runs some very successful campaigns, many of them based in HNWI. That said, not all their prospects arrive with major gifts. According to Jerry Panas, one of the USA's leading fundraising consultants, when Harvard did a study after its last campaign, of its 254 million-dollar donors, it found two out of three started with first-time gifts of $100 or less. Harvard's secret is to engage some small-value supporters and work them up to become major prospects.

Part of the solution to the problem of pricing your proposition is a gift table. If you're an experienced professional fundraiser, you are familiar with major campaign gift tables showing the number of donations needed at each level to deliver an overall campaign goal.

Figure 2.5 shows a gift table we prepared for a campaign we designed. As well as the number of gifts needed, it also details the number of prospects needed at each level, plus the number needed at two different likely ratios of success. With *warm prospects*, you have an existing positive relationship. With *cold prospects*, you don't. Warm prospects are more likely to convert to donors, which means you need fewer of them.

Gift amount	Gifts needed	Prospects needed (warm – 4:1)	Prospects needed (cold – 9:1)
£500,000	2	8	18
£250,000	2	8	18
£125,000	4	16	36
£50,000	8	32	72
£25,000	12	48	108
£10,000	25	100	225
£5,000	50	200	450
Total	103	412	927

Figure 2.5: Sample gift table

This is a useful internal framework. If you are approaching a number of people for support, you should be clear about the category into which you think your prospect or prospects might fit. But never show this table to a prospect. It reduces their sense of agency and might even make them feel more like another brick in the donor wall than a valued supporter.

When planning your table, begin by thinking of the impact each gift level could have, and how you might reward or fulfil the donor. We sometimes start with as little as £1. But for major gift projects you might begin at £1,000 and move up to £10,000, £100,000, £1 million, £10 million and even £100 million.

Table 2.1 shows an example for the amazing MEF palaeontological museum in Trelew, Patagonia[4] to help them raise the money to house the largest dinosaur ever found – and the largest creature ever to walk on land. The problem for MEF was that it had discovered a three-storey dinosaur and only had a two-storey museum.[5] We had two challenges. One was to identify specific prospects who were interested in dinosaurs and palaeontology (not a big data set). The other was to find donors who would be interested in other aspects of their work to do with the environment, natural history, Argentinian heritage, education, local economics and so on. Or indeed donors interested in self or corporate promotions, signalling their pride in their nationality.

Table 2.1: Fundraising for the MEF palaeontological museum in Trelew, Patagonia

Gift level US$	Impact	Fulfilment
1 million	Invest the sum needed to assemble and display the skeleton of the largest creature ever to walk the earth. Make this amazing spectacle available for all the world to visit.	The chance to unveil the dinosaur at the museum reopening plus all the associated media exposure. The gallery where the dinosaur is housed will be named after you for 10 years and you will have unique entertainment opportunities in the gallery for that period.
500,000	Create a whole new gallery in the museum, themed in one of several ways by geological age or	Have a themed exhibit named after you, your loved one or company for five years.

---

[4] https://mef.org.ar/home.
[5] If you want to know more, Google some of the videos David Attenborough has made about the museum.

	by issue – such as the effect of previous climate changes.	The opportunity to have entertainment events in the gallery with family, friends or business contacts.
250,000	Support the development of young academics in Argentina. Meet the salary and on-costs for a scholarship PhD student to work on research for five years.	Enjoy a personally guided field trip in Patagonia with the possibility of finding new discoveries of fossils. The scholarship will be named in your honour.
100,000	Bring the best in global visiting research talent. Meet the salary and on-costs for a senior international museum professional researcher for 12 months.	Enjoy a personal guided tour of the museum with the brilliant CEO and the chance for a dinner and drinks reception in your honour.
50,000	Grow our young people in the district. Pay for the education programme to involve 10 local schools in the museum's Discovery Programmes for 12 months.	Have the schools programme named after you and the chance to meet the children and young people. We will help with local TV and radio coverage.
25,000	Allow everyone to enjoy the past and find out about the future. Ensure that a specific class of local children with special needs can enjoy field trips to discover dinosaurs.	Receive a 'thank you' video message from the young people and their teachers while on the trip.
15,000	Give us the tools to make new discoveries. Invest in a scanner that allows palaeontologists to look inside rock samples and detect fossils.	Receive a small fossil specially mounted on a plaque to have in your home or office.
5,000	Ensure your name or the name of someone you love is encased in history. Pay for a small fossil to be preserved, mounted and displayed in the museum for five years.	Have your contribution recognised on a small plaque next to the fossil displayed.
1,000	Share the learning. Meet the cost of a school trip to the museum for a class of 40 underprivileged children to visit, including transport, lunches and take-home education packs.	Have your contribution as a local philanthropist recognised on a supporters' board at the museum entrance.

Note that this version of the table was an early draft. The final version has some – confidential – changes.

Under Tool 8: Check for (sticky) SUCCESS, we'll explore how to present these options in an engaging way.

To create a really powerful proposition, you need to match the prospect's interests as far as possible. You can see that Table 2.1 frames individual gifts around different concerns about:

- opportunities for young people

- honouring loved ones

- access for excluded groups

- safeguarding precious palaeontological discoveries

- maintaining scientific standards

- personal or corporate promotion

- entertainment or PR opportunities.

Ideally, when you meet a prospect with an idea about their specific focus you should aim to have between three and five options, all with a different bias towards their interest – such as heritage, education, science and learning.

 Top tip: Some don'ts

- DON'T have a massive list of 20–30 options on display in a big Excel spreadsheet. If you do, you run the risk of cognitive – choice – overload.

This can make a prospect back away and even do nothing. You can always offer other options if the three to five you have on the table don't work.

- DON'T forget that forever is a long time. Notice how all the MEF opportunities have a time limit on them. Think about how long any fulfilment will last. If you offer a naming in perpetuity, it can seriously hinder the potential for future fundraisers.

- DON'T be so obsessed with your own offer that you don't hear when an apparently reluctant donor is telling you what they are interested in – see the Be Prepared case study below.

Also think about what you call your table. Increasingly, fundraisers are moving away from calling it a gift opportunity ladder or table, instead referring to an 'impact ladder'. This simple change in language can make a massive difference. Prospects are choosing the impact they want to have, not the level of donation they want to make.

Finally, be aware that you may begin your engagement journey with a 'discovery' call or a discovery visit where you don't present any proposition whatsoever. Instead, the conversation would be entirely about the supporter or prospect, their interests and seeking a clue to their propensity to give.[6]

---

[6] Try suggesting a significant gift beyond what your research suggests to see what's possible. You may get a negative reaction – so what should

Top tip: Be prepared

No matter how ready you are, you need to always be prepared to respond to a transformational opportunity in the room. We are big fans of the super smart Marina Jones at the Royal Opera House in London. She gives a great example of meeting with a trustee of a foundation. She and her team had done the research, and had been introduced by two members of her development committee to the trustee and the foundation. All the information she had suggested her best bet was to pitch for a £20,000–£30,000 gift. When she met the trustee after an initial discussion, he announced that the foundation was planning to spend out – that is, close down. He wanted to know what they could do with a gift of £1 million+. Marina calmly signalled she would come back with some clear propositions. And she did, securing £1.85 million.

Anchor your offer

In Chapter 1, we talked about giving yourself a positive emotional anchor. Behavioural science teaches us you can

---

you do? Here's good advice from the excellent Canadian fundraiser Guy Mallabone. He has a great way of watching carefully to see how the prospect reacts as he signals a potential stretch gift. If the prospect looks nonplussed, Guy quickly follows up with, 'I realise that's a lot, but I wanted to honour your commitment to the cause, which I know is strong. We can always talk about other options.'

also use a version of anchoring with prospects, where the very first stimulus to which they are exposed functions as a mental anchor. (In this case, the anchor is more of a reference point.) For example, in a commercial setting – say, a clothes shop – displaying a label on a garment with a previous higher price and highlighting a 'current' reduced price engenders a sense of 'bargain' in the customer, even if the price paid in the end isn't, objectively, a good deal. People will simply judge the discount price using the 'original' price as the anchor. They may even focus solely on saving 50%. It sounds so good – even if hardly anyone ever paid the 100%.

Anchoring is a kind of priming – see Tool 13: Try philanthropic pre-suasion – prime for success in Chapter 4. It's a key bias through which what Daniel Kahneman calls System 1 exercises control over System 2 (see Preface) without individuals being aware of it.

As a fundraiser, this means that when you approach a prospect, you might find a way early on of letting them know that other donors have already contributed at a specific significant level – let's say £20,000. Within certain constraints, if you do this you're more likely to secure a larger gift than you would without this anchor. As well as an anchor, this also helps with what is called *social proof* – the tendency people have to follow what they believe to be the norms as set by others. The introduction of the higher value gift 'anchor' creates a reference point for any subsequent discussion or decision. Seems improbable? Here's an example from a face-to-face street fundraising experiment we organised in New York City.

Testing anchors in New York City

In October 2019, after delivering a brief training session on some of the core influence techniques – including anchoring – to a team of 23 experienced face-to-face fundraisers, we worked with them for the rest of the day on the streets of New York City.

To demonstrate the anchoring effect, we asked the fundraisers to approach people where the street number was prominent, and to actively refer to it, saying something like, 'Wow this is a lucky corner here on 43rd Street.' The purpose was to see whether mentioning the street number had a positive effect on the size of gift. And it did. The average gift solicited on the street is a monthly commitment of about $30 a month. Standing next to the sign and mentioning the street number – such as the example of 43rd Street in Figure 2.6 – increased the average gift to $38 a month.

Figure 2.6: Face-to-face fundraising on 43rd street

Why does this work? Daniel Kahneman says people find it hard to make a decision in a vacuum. They need something – a benchmark or a reference point – against which to compare their choice. This is especially true when they make a decision that involves numbers, such as buying something or making a donation. Often the reference point comes from past experience: 'I usually buy X for Y amount' or 'We normally donate Z every month'. But when a person is in unfamiliar territory, it's helpful to them – and to you – to provide a starting point that makes the decision easier. It gives the prospect a mental shortcut and appeals to their lazy System 1 brain – and it also increases your fundraising success. The anchor is that reference point.

This works with larger gifts in exactly the same way. By mentioning that the average proposition might involve a commitment of, say, £300,000, you are setting the mental counter of the prospect in that ballpark. You can use the impact ladder to help you with this by putting the £300,000 item at the centre point of your list. Yes, we really are biased to pick middle options.

Tool 8:
Check for (sticky) SUCCESS

When to use it: People forget most of what they hear and see very quickly. You need to use the SUCCESS tool whenever you have an idea that you need prospects to find interesting *and* memorable.

Practice grade: 2

Once you have the basic proposal set up, you need to run your proposition and story arc through the SUCCESS checklist to make sure it is 'sticky' – that is, that it will arouse interest and stay in people's minds. Stickiness is important because people remember as little as 5% of the material to which they are exposed after 24 hours.

The human tendency to forget lots of information quickly was first studied by the German scientist Herman Ebbinghaus. He captured findings in a graph showing what has become known as the Ebbinghaus effect. The typical curve that Ebbinghaus created for remembering/forgetting is shown in Figure 2.7.

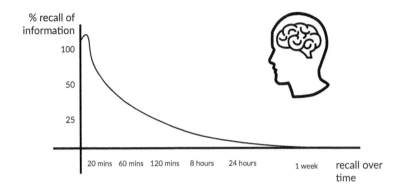

Figure 2.7: The Ebbinghaus effect

Notice that immediately after exposure to any information, there is a slight increase in the ability to remember as our brains sort stuff away. After that brief burst of activity, though, over the next 24 hours we rapidly lose access to key ideas and messages. Ebbinghaus reckoned that we retain as little as 5% of the information we receive 24 hours later. Why does this happen? Well, if you think about it, our brains would quickly be overwhelmed if we tried to remember everything to which we were exposed.

Clearly, it's critical to make sure your idea is in the 5% that's retained. If you're not convinced about the level of decay, here's a little thought experiment. Think about any advertisements you saw while watching TV, web browsing or reading the newspaper last night. How many can you remember? And how specifically? In other words, can you go beyond topic to the actual brand? It's quite a sobering thought for the car company that shelled out £550,000 to make the ad and £50,000 to broadcast it... but you can't remember which car was being promoted. Also notice that you may remember some fairly random things from the advert – like the lyric of the song playing in the background or (to go back a bit) the names of the characters in the advert – Nicole and Papa… If you think about it, you can remember some pretty random things in your life – old phone numbers, former post – or zip – codes, the words to a song you last heard 20 years ago, the smell of the polish your granny used. Memory is very complex.

Yet there are ideas that seem to very quickly and easily acquire significant, massive circulation and stay in people's memories. These ideas are sticky. Some are natural – that is, they have grown up seemingly spontaneously. And some have consciously been designed by advertising executives, marketers, advocacy specialists or even charity fundraisers.

We can find sticky ideas everywhere. The Heath Brothers – authors of the brilliant *Made to Stick*[7] – were drawn to this area through an interest in questions such as what makes 'urban legends' – like the myth that the Great Wall of China is the only human-made object visible from space – so compelling? How do some teachers make what could be mundane chemistry or geography lessons work much better than others? Why do some slogans – 'Get Brexit done', 'A dog is for life not just for Christmas' – stick in the mind?

The brothers came up with a framework to help ensure stickiness based around the mnemonic SUCCESS. You need to make sure your proposal – your case for support – tells a story and that the story both creates an immediate impact and remains memorable. SUCCESS is about the elements in

---

[7] Chip Heath and Dan Heath, *Made to Stick: Why Some Ideas Survive and Others Die* (2007).

your story, and where possible it meets six key principles: it should be a Simple, Unexpected, Concrete, Credible, and Emotional Story – and we've added a seventh, Simply told. Yes, simplicity is so important we've used it twice. With this formula, you can shape your story and make it powerful and sticky so it stays in your prospect's mind. Remember, even if is not competing with advertisements, and work or social information – it's probably competing with other fundraising propositions from other excellent causes. (If you've found this prospect, there's a good chance another fundraiser has also found them.) SUCCESS in this concentration contest comes from:

S   Simple: identify your core message and make it short and sweet.

U   Unexpected: engage and intrigue your prospect with counterintuitive ideas.

C   Concrete: make it real – the prospect needs to see, smell and touch the idea.

C   Credible: use detail and information that supports your idea.

E   Emotional: evoke and attach feelings about what is important.

S   Story: make the idea easy to remember and relatable by embedding it in a story.

S   Simply told: repeated by us to make sure you remove all unnecessary information.

Principle 1: Simple

Many of the most memorable messages are, not surprisingly, the shortest. That's why politicians use slogans. President

Trump's 2016 election message, 'Make America Great Again', and the UK government's first Covid-19 lockdown message, 'Stay home, protect the NHS, save lives', come to mind. Advertisements are great at this – think 'Beanz Meanz Heinz', 'Diamonds are Forever' or 'Every Little Helps'.

Think of $e=mc^2$. Along with H_2O, this is possibly the best-known scientific formula on the planet. The implications of $e=mc^2$ are wide ranging, counter-intuitive and outside most of our understanding. But by summarising complex work in an equation for fellow scientists, Einstein also managed to make it memorable for everyone.

To strip an idea down to its core, we need to pare away all the extras and prioritise the key elements. Saying something in few words is not the goal – 'sound bites' or slogans are not what we're suggesting. That said, proverbs are an interesting format. 'Look before you leap' has some real wisdom in it as well as being a catchy line.

The aim is to create supportable ideas that are both simple and profound.

Principle 2: Unexpected

How do you persuade your audience to pay *attention*, and how do you keep their *interest* when it will take time to get the ideas across? You need to disrupt people's expectations.

It is essential to avoid the 'blah blah blah' message, which causes audiences to tune out because they're (over-)familiar and perhaps a little bored with it. Some painful examples for those of us who care might be 'People in developing nations don't have access to proper medical facilities'; 'The planet's climate is changing, and human activity is responsible'; and 'People with drug addiction need support and help, not punishment'. For many people – even supporters – these messages become static in the background and they tune out.

To disrupt this blah blah blah mindset, you may need to be disruptive – that is, approach communicating ideas in a radically different way, or tackle popular misconceptions head on. By doing this, you gain attention – or 'headshare'. In a moment of genius, Bill Gates put aside the PowerPoint and podium at a fundraising event and released a slew of mosquitoes into a room filled with millionaire donors. His goal was to engage them in the campaign to buy mosquito nets for children in sub-Saharan Africa. As the astonished audience swatted at thousands of whining insects, Gates' message, 'Now you know what it's like. Provide a net for the kids', was truly driven home.

Another way to disrupt a mindset is to challenge an 'accepted fact' in your story. For example, a UK refugee organisation began a presentation by telling people that Britain was, in fact, a nation of net emigrants – more UK citizens settle overseas every year than people enter the UK. That countered the traditional view reported in the conservative media that Britain was being 'flooded with foreigners'. The implication? If we're against immigration we need to stop Britons going abroad, rather than worry about people coming in.

You can also use 'mystery' to increase alertness and grab people's attention. There's a great example of a fundraiser[8] for a youth employment charity who asked his corporate

---

[8] Our hero fundraiser and friend is too modest to want his name used, and we're respecting that.

sponsors for more money so the organisation could apparently do less well. He began by showing the room of sponsors a slide illustrating how their contributions in the previous two years had led to a 10% and then a 25% increase in the number of young people the charity had reached. He then asked for another £5 million for the coming year. And paused. The audience waited for the next slide, assuming a new graph would show the even greater impact to come. The expectation was to see a 35% or even a 50% increase. There were gasps when what he in fact revealed was a graph showing that in exchange for their additional £5 million, the number of young people reached would go down – by 20%. The corporate bosses were puzzled, and intrigued. Had there been a mistake? More money... but worse results? Pausing again for effect, our friend the fundraiser went on to explain:

> The only way we can carry on reaching young people at the rate we've been doing for the last two years is if we work with the easiest-to-reach ones. Next year, we'd like to focus on the really difficult-to-reach young people – maybe those involved in crime or addiction. Reaching them is more difficult and more expensive. And to be honest we need to be more innovative in our work, and to take more risks in our programmes. We can't just be in the 'easy to reach' game. We'd like your support to try to bring in those very at-risk young people. That's why I'm asking for more money to reach fewer people.

This certainly made the audience sit up, as like most sponsors they had expected that an increase in their contributions would lead to better results. But the explanation caught their attention and made sense. By introducing the idea of the importance of innovation, and the risks associated with it, the fundraiser captured their attention. (Oh, and he got the money!)

But surprise and mystery don't last forever. For your idea to endure in the long term, you need to generate some additional responses such as interest and curiosity. You can do this in your conversation or presentation by 'opening gaps' in the prospect's knowledge, then filling – or getting them to fill in – those gaps. You're looking for headshare.

Principle 3: Concrete

To make your ideas clear and understandable, make them visceral – explain them in terms of human actions and the senses by which we find out about these actions – vision, words, smell, taste, etc. This is where so much business and charity communication goes wrong. Way too many mission statements, strategies and visions are ambiguous, or vague, or general to the point of being meaningless.

Naturally sticky ideas are full of concrete images – because our brains are wired to remember concrete data. Notice again how proverbs contain abstract truths couched in concrete language: 'A bird in the hand is worth two in the bush.'

You can even make a group of people experience a concrete feeling. A Mexican domestic violence charity with which we worked held a dinner for donors on an empty piece of land it had acquired. Marked on the bare site with plastic tape and nails was the outline shape of the refuge the charity hoped to build. The meal was held in the 'imaginary' building. It was a barbecue done in the family style, symbolising that the prospects were the 'family' who were to build this house for women who had been abused by their partners.

After the meal, walking carefully between the tape lines as if they were real walls, the prospects were given a 'guided tour' of the imaginary building. They talked with the refuge staff and among themselves about the facilities they could 'see' in their imaginations. Several of the prospects commented that the rooms laid out on the ground looked too small. They asked how much it would cost to make the rooms bigger so the women arriving in the refuge and their children would have more space. Others noticed that the showers and toilets were shared. They asked about the cost to provide each woman with her own shower and toilet. By getting the prospects to stand in the imagined physical space, rather than looking at the architect's plans, the charity was able to put the prospects into the problem and allow them to choose to solve it. They went on to commit to build what they had 'seen'. That refuge now exists.

Speaking or writing tangibly – and ideally putting prospects 'into' the situation – is the perfect way to ensure that your idea will impact everyone in your audience. For more on this, see Tool 17: Pivot perceptual positions – choose another angle in Chapter 5.

This concrete approach also helps enormously with making your message memorable. Think about the story of the *Titanic* – what do you remember? It's the concrete details: the hubris behind the claim the ship was 'unsinkable', the band playing on as it sank, women and children leaving first, the captain going down with his ship, etc. These details make it come alive.

Find a killer number and attach it to a story: World Wide Fund for Nature

Working with the WWF to illustrate how vulnerable wildlife is to poaching in Africa, we came up with this example:

> Notch is the name of one of the last three breeding female white rhinos in Botswana. If she mistakenly wanders from her natural habitat in Botswana across the border into Zimbabwe, on average a rhino like Notch has only 32 minutes to live. Why? In her home in Botswana there is wildlife security and protection. In Zimbabwe, poachers haunt the border looking for elephants and rhinos, without a good sense of the danger across international boundaries. The poachers will kill as many of these elephants and rhinos as they can find, and cut out their tusks or horn to sell, leaving the carcasses to rot. We need your help to station game guardians on the border and to electronically tag Notch. We need her to live more than 32 minutes. We need to save Notch and her calves. We need to save the species.

People remember the 32 minutes and the name of the rhino – Notch. It's much more memorable than saying '22% of rhinos are poached each year. They are at danger from poachers.'

A single hero and one powerful statistic can be very compelling.

Principle 4: Credible

How do you help people believe in your ideas? When the head of the British Medical Association talks about a public health issue, such as smoking being bad for you, most people accept this without scepticism. But in day-to-day situations, the rest of us don't enjoy this authority. And sadly, in this age of anti-experts who produce 'alternative facts', even a respected and respectable scientist or academic may struggle to get their views across.

Sticky ideas have to carry their own credentials. You need ways to help people test them out – without piling on the statistics. When trying to build a case, most fundraisers instinctively grasp for hard numbers and lots of data. But often this is exactly the wrong approach. Rather, as the Heath Brothers say, use the 'try before you buy' approach.

In the only US presidential debate in 1980 between Ronald Reagan and Jimmy Carter, Reagan could have cited innumerable statistics demonstrating the sluggishness of the US economy. Instead, he posed a question to which the majority of voters apparently had the same answer. 'Before you vote, ask yourself if you are better off today than you were four years ago.' Voters decided that the answer was 'no'. And Ronald Reagan came into the White House... Think also of the 2016 UK Brexit referendum where one giant lie of a number on the side of a bus, 'An extra £350M a week to spend on the NHS', was successfully used as a key reason to vote for Brexit.

Ideally you need a killer number – a true one rather than one that has been made up – that sticks in people's minds and captures their attention.

Try the pratfall effect to improve credibility

At all costs avoid *Stepford Wives* syndrome,[9] where your annual report or webpage becomes a channel to claim that all your programmes and processes have worked perfectly over the last year. If you admit to some weaknesses or failures, it will help significantly with your credibility. This is the pratfall effect in action. Put simply, behavioural science research tells us we don't trust perfection. It doesn't seem authentic. The effect has been documented in Amazon, where products with a perfect 5* rating tend not to be as trusted as those with a score of 4.5 and one or two negative reviews.

The phenomenon was first studied by social psychologist Elliot Aronson in 1966. Aronson asked a presenter to give the same talk twice to different audiences. The first time, he asked the presenter to deliver the talk perfectly. The second time, he asked the presenter to accidentally spill some water on himself from a glass before starting. The presenter was asked to acknowledge his clumsiness and then go on to deliver the presentation as before. What was interesting was that the audience scored the version with the 'mistake' as more trustworthy information and scored the presenter as more likeable and

---

[9] This movie, *The Stepford Wives*, involves a community where all the wives are 'perfect'. The original version from the 1970s is darker and more sinister than the remake, but the premise is the same – nothing that seems 'perfect' can be true. And the illusion of perfection makes people uneasy. Real life is messy, and we have to acknowledge that in our communications.

credible. This effect suggests that people or organisations normally considered highly competent are more likeable and credible when they make and admit to a small mistake.

How often have you felt frustrated by a company you feel has let you down in some way, and heard yourself say, 'If only they would admit they had made a mistake and say sorry.' Don't be afraid to admit to a failed programme or project – within reason.

Principle 5: Emotional

If you want people to care about your ideas, think first about the emotions you want to generate – joy, sadness, anger, frustration, surprise, fear…?

For example, you may want to make prospects angry about how victims of domestic violence are ignored by the legal system. Or sad about how many women are harmed. Or frightened that if they were the victims of abuse there would be nowhere for them to go. (Note that it's often a feeling that creates action – the word is e-motion. That's what you're aiming for.)

Research shows that people are more likely to make a charitable gift to a single needy individual than to an entire impoverished region or nation – or even a small group. We seem to be hard-wired to feel things for an identifiable person, not for abstractions. Paul Slovic, Professor of Psychology at the University of Oregon and the President of Decision Research, has demonstrated this by measuring the donation levels from people shown pictures of children in distress as part of a charity fundraising drive. Some subjects saw a photo of a single distressed child from Mali, while others were shown a photo of two children in similar terrible condition. To ensure the comparison was fair, the photos were from the same angle, and the children were the same age and appearance to the individual child. All were given a name.

The subjects shown two children donated 15% less than those shown a single child. That's right: the single child attracted higher donations.

In a related experiment, subjects shown a group of eight starving children contributed 50% less money than those shown just one. Slovic called this the collapse of compassion – illustrated in Figure 2.8. As Mother Teresa said, 'If I look at the mass, I will never act. If I look at the one, I will.' The reasons for this response are complex, but there seems to be some relationship to the idea of agency – I can maybe help one person, but I feel powerless to help more than one.

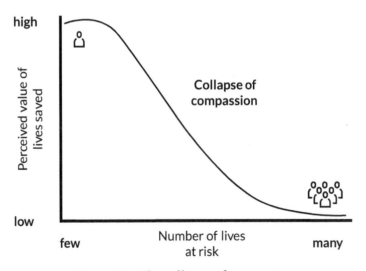

Figure 2.8: The collapse of compassion

We personally find this result distressing, but it contains useful learning. Make your stories focus on individuals if you want to drive action. Does this mean that when you're with a major donor you should only ask for support for one person? No, but it does mean you should illustrate the bigger cause you need support for *through a single focus*. This could be the story of one student (representing thousands) denied the chance for higher education through poverty, or one activist (representing hundreds) arrested for campaigning for human rights, or one woman (representing dozens) unable to find a safe refuge when she fled her abusive partner.

You also need to consider what's the best or rather most appropriate emotion to engage – anger, fear, pride, love…? Another study demonstrates how difficult it is to get teenagers to stop smoking by talking about the negative long-term consequences. (Remember how focused we are as a species on short-term impacts?) It is much easier – and more effective – to tap into their resentment of the deceit practised on them by big business – specifically tobacco corporations.

Principle 6: Story

How do you get people to remember and act on your ideas? You need to make sure you tell a proper story – not just an anecdote. Newspaper reporters know how to bring a situation alive even when they don't have the images that TV news has. Look at this example adapted from the novel *The Shipping News* by Annie Proulx. It's a conversation between Quoyle, the novel's protagonist, and the publisher of the local newspaper.

Publisher: It's finding the centre of your story, the beating heart of it, that's what makes a reporter. You have to start by making up some headlines. You know: short, punchy, dramatic headlines. Now, have a look [pointing at dark clouds gathering in the sky over the ocean], what do you see? Tell me the headline.

Protagonist: HORIZON FILLS WITH DARK CLOUDS

Publisher: IMMINENT STORM THREATENS VILLAGE

Protagonist: But what if no storm comes?

Publisher: VILLAGE SPARED FROM DEADLY STORM

Aid workers, firefighters and soldiers naturally swap stories after an emergency situation, a fire or a battle. By doing this, they multiply and share their experiences, looking for resonance and commonality. Stories have a very specific purpose for many professionals – they become an informal system of knowledge management. After years of hearing stories, the people they are designed for have a richer, more complete mental catalogue of critical situations they might confront and the appropriate responses. UNICEF has hired storytellers to help improve its knowledge management and the senior campaigner in Greenpeace is now called Head of Storytelling. At =mc we worked with Oxfam to create board games based around stories that captured and codified the learning that experienced staff had of working in emergency relief situations.

Research shows that mentally rehearsing a situation in the form of a story helps us perform better when we actually encounter it. Similarly, hearing appropriate stories acts as a kind of mental flight simulator, preparing us to respond more quickly and effectively. Stories are an ancestral way of sharing culture, experiences and values from which we can learn. Rather than giving your prospect lots of statistics, tell them a story that incorporates the values and achievements you want them to remember. Think back over the book so far – what do you remember…? The Pele story? The Notch the Rhino story?

Finally, stories are a way to celebrate your organisation's heroes – they are a great guide to culture. Think about the stories where you work. Who are they about – the CEO, the frontliner, the volunteer, the supporter? What do they celebrate – imagination, risk taking, user/supporter care, investment? Make sure the story you share celebrates the person and the values you want to champion. Remember, too, the story you want the prospect to be able to share. Put as much energy into that as your own story.

Principle 7: Simply told

We've repeated 'simple' and made it up to a seventh principle for two reasons. First, simple is so important that it's worth repeating. Make your message as simple as possible – like Picasso's series of drawings of a bull that begins as a detailed sketch and then eventually becomes only eight lines… or Einstein's formula, $e=mc^2$. Both are the essence of simplicity, yet both also convey complex ideas. Simple is not the same as simplistic.

Second, to fix something in the brain, it's helpful to repeat it in a memorable way. Using the SUCCESS acronym helps make the formula itself memorable.

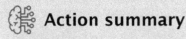 **Action summary**

It's vital that you prepare your proposal well and in a range of ways that make it easy to adapt to the format you need and to the individual or agency you are going to share it with.

✓ Begin by creating the big picture – your case for support. Shape it using the =mc story arc framework – how could you present this as a risk, a crisis, and opportunity and a vision? Notice that one of these options will probably appeal more to the prospect than the others. And different prospects may prefer different options.

✓ Build into your story someone the prospect can empathise or identify with – a hero. Where you can, make the prospect the hero. Give them a story to tell about how they helped to save refugees from floods, or brought theatre to young people, or saved the ancient manuscript from decay.

✓ Chunk up your case, and the big investment needed to make it happen, into propositions – manageable pieces of philanthropy based around the prospect's money and motivation.

✓ Make your idea memorable and impactful using the SUCCESS checklist: a Simple Unexpected Concrete Credible Emotional Story – Simply told. Apply as many of these elements to your proposal as you can to help make it sticky.

By the way, what's the name of that Great Northern White rhino you'd love to save? And how long is she likely to live if she wanders over the border into Zimbabwe?

Chapter 3

Preparation

By failing to prepare, you are preparing to fail.

Benjamin Franklin

It's great to be charming, clever and 'quick on your feet'. These are all qualities with which some lucky people are born. But even people fortunate enough to have these qualities are rarely able to deliver *consistent* results. For consistent results, you need to be excellent at preparation – thinking through a whole range of possible outcomes and how you might handle them. Key here is preparing to be more flexible and not to prepare a script.

In this chapter, we'll look at four tools that will help you prepare better and more comprehensively, so then whatever the prospect throws at you, you'll be ready and able to adapt. The key tools in *Preparation* are:

- Identify what the well-formed outcome is that you want.

- Establish your LIM-it – your best, acceptable and least favoured options.

- Create a receptive state in others using flexible frames.

- Establish the key think, feel, do sequence to roll out your idea.

Figure 3.1: The preparation power tools

Outcome before means or moves

Some fundraisers are obsessed with moves management – an old-fashioned mechanistic approach focused on deciding what you want the prospect to do next, and next, and so on – and what you should do to persuade them – for example, write them an email, ask for a meeting, make a call.

In our experience, you need to start with an outcome – the result you want: the *what*. From that, the *how* should follow.

We're encouraging you to focus on outcome not methodology to help you be more flexible. If you're specific about what you want at the outset, you can then concentrate on building flexibility into your approach. If one way doesn't work, try another.

The term 'well-formed outcome' was originally developed in neuro-linguistic programming (NLP), an approach to self-development that has some uses (though in our view it's massively oversold). The outcome is more than simply a goal – 'to secure the gift'. To be a well-formed outcome, it has to achieve certain criteria, which mean it will:

- be within your power to deliver

- avoid unintended costs or consequences

- address any internal conflicts – feelings or thoughts – about the outcome.

Tool 9:
Develop a well-formed outcome

When to use it: Use this as a way of clearly identifying what success will mean to you and to the project – and use this clarity to identify the most effective route to secure that result.

Practice grade: 4

Seven steps to establish the outcome you want

A successful outcome must fit your needs and interests as well as the prospect's. To prepare for that result we suggest seven steps:

Step 1: Be clear about your goal.

Step 2: Establish the evidence.

Step 3: Consider the context.

Step 4: Establish your resources.

Step 5: Consider the consequences.

Step 6: Anticipate challenges.

Step 7: Take the first step.

Step 1: Be clear about your goal

Many fundraisers tend to go into asking situations too vague about what exactly it is they want – for example, 'To get a substantial gift', or 'To engage Ms. Jones in the cause.'

To clarify your outcome effectively, make sure it's positive and specific.

Positive

An outcome described in positive terms is more powerful than one described in negative terms, yet we often approach a meeting thinking 'I hope I don't say the wrong thing' or 'I really don't want to appear nervous'. The result is that we make the very mistake we're hoping to avoid.

 Top tip: Your brain ignores negative injunctions

If we say to you 'Don't think about bananas', what immediately pops into your head? It's not, by any chance, a picture of a curved fruit – yellow skin, soft interior? There's an important psychological principle at work here. Your brain is not very good at recognising and responding to negatives, which means it often deletes words like 'don't' – leaving you with '(Don't) think of a banana…' This phenomenon also helps explain why people often have challenges with life goals such as 'I must not eat French fries' or 'I need to give up smoking'. The negative element in the goals – 'stop' and 'give up' are misted over by the brain, leaving 'I must eat fries' and 'I need to smoke'.

Instead of expressing your outcome as 'Prevent this donor leaving the board', try 'Get the donor to recommit to a three-year term'. Or instead of 'Not screw up and get no gift', try 'Ensure the prospect wants to consider a proposal'.

Specific

The outcome you describe must be sufficiently concrete to keep you focused on it and for it to represent a possible achievement. It should be neither too modest nor a fantasy. To help develop a stretch goal, you might imagine the prospect saying, 'Well, that's a gift way beyond what I had thought about. But after the way you've explained the difference a gift like this might make, I'm thinking I should consider that.'

Specific doesn't mean unchangeable – you can adapt the outcome if it proves unrealistic. But specific beats vague every time. In 1954, the UK athlete Roger Bannister set himself the goal 'to run a four-minute mile,' not 'to run as fast as I can'. The specification of the four-minute mile gave Bannister a very clear focus against which all his improvements (and setbacks) could be measured on the road to success. The more concretely you can imagine your goal or outcome, the more achievable it will be.

Step 2: Establish the evidence

In creating a positive, concrete outcome, you begin the process of preparing yourself for success. (Think of it as loading up another useful piece of mental software.) To complete the process, you need to think about the modality and the metrics. The modality is about how you will experience success in terms of seeing, hearing and feeling – technically called sensory systems. The metrics are the specific measures or indicators of success. Together, they work as shown in Table 3.1.

Table 3.1: Mental metrics

Modality	Mental metrics
Seeing	What will you see when you succeed? A smiling prospect walking towards you? An outstretched hand shaking on the deal? A thoughtful expression that turns to a smile as they make a difficult decision in your favour?
Hearing	What will you hear? The prospect saying 'Yes!' in an excited tone? A softly spoken offer to consider the proposition? Clapping as others in your team applaud your success when you report back?
Feeling	What will you feel? Excited at the shake of the prospect's hand? Relieved as you sit back in a soft chair in the prospect's home after hearing the news? Pleasure as you reflect on the terrific impact the gift will deliver?

Imagining what success will be like as exactly as possible is a powerful technique to orientate your action and behaviour. Success is also important for your prospect. Make sure you spend time thinking about what they will see, feel and hear (and, of course, the DOSE neurochemicals these senses will stimulate). In this way, you can help them to achieve their outcome – which should, of course, complement yours.

Create future history: Learn from The Greatest

As you'll be aware from reading Chapter 1, a well-formed outcome is a variant on the anchoring technique used by lots of athletes. From football penalty takers to golf pros, athletes are systematically coached to mentally rehearse not just the contest but also the win.[1] Like many fundraisers, they have just one chance to get it right. Note the difference here. Instead of looking to recreate a state based on a powerful past experience, they are trying to create a future reality so strong it almost becomes a kind of future memory.

The champion boxer Muhammad Ali – formerly Cassius Clay – did this instinctively in the 1960s and 1970s, well before the neuroscience and psychology were fully understood. Considered not only by himself but by many boxing fans as The Greatest, he used to mentally rehearse all his fights – and the outcome – before the event. He called this rehearsal creating 'future history'. To do this, he would change into his boxing gear before the contest and literally act out the fight in his hotel bedroom, imagining how it would go almost blow by blow. At the moment of his imagined victory, he would then carefully 'anchor' – or embed in his consciousness – the result he'd conjured up. Often this would be a knock-down punch. At that moment, he saw the flash of the photographers' camera bulbs recording his success, he heard the crowd chanting his name and he felt his triumph – even smelling his

---

[1] The technique is used by artists too – ballet dancers will often use visualisation as a means to recover from injury.

own sweat as the imaginary referee lifted his right arm in victory. Too weird? Not for Ali.

He would go further and make up an aphoristic poem to capture the memory, such as 'Clay swings with a right, what a beautiful swing, And raises the bear straight out of the ring'. Before his 1964 fight with Sonny Liston, he made up one of his most famous poems: 'Float like a butterfly, sting like a bee – his hands can't hit what his eyes can't see'. Before the Rumble in the Jungle with George Foreman in 1974, Ali went into the ring psyched up to win and with the exact metrics and modality programmed into his brain. You need to create your future history of a successful ask.

How can you establish your sense of what success might be like and develop your own modality and mental metrics for success? Table 3.2 contains some suggestions to help get you started.

Table 3.2: Suggestions for mental metrics

Modality	Mental metrics
What does success look like? (Think about Muhammad Ali – he imagines the flash of the photographers' bulbs as they capture him succeeding.)	What do you see when you succeed – a smile, a cheque, a handshake? Who's there in your success picture – you, other donors, beneficiaries? What are the details of the setting where this takes place – a house, your office, a project?
What does success sound like? (Ali hears the sound of the crowd chanting his name as a tribute to his victory, 'Ali, Ali, Ali, Ali!')	What do you hear when you succeed? What is said? Who says it? What do you say? In what kind of tone is agreement reached – upbeat and excited or more reflective and considered? Do the words come fast or slow?

What does success feel like and what are the physical sensations?	What feelings do you have? Happy, proud, excited, relieved...? What feelings does the donor have – anxious but excited, passionate, in touch with their values? If there's a handshake between you, is it firm and slow or fast and excited?
(Ali smells his sweat when he has mentally 'won'. Smell is a powerful aid to changing your emotional state. Ali also feels emotion as he acknowledges the crowd.)	

Notice the examples are all in the present tense – not what *will* happen but what *is* happening – as though that moment of success is now. Muhammad Ali didn't say 'I could be the greatest...'; he said 'I am the greatest.'

You need to collect and programme evidence into your brain on what success is like so you'll know when you've succeeded. There are two kinds of useful evidence:

- *End result evidence.* What will ultimate success – the result you want – be like? The verbal commitment to the gift? Reading the email agreeing to make the investment? The feeling of a tough job done?

- *Milestone evidence.* What will success en route be like? Getting off the phone having successfully made the appointment? Presenting the case for support and the prospect asking positive questions? Feeling that you've established a rapport?

Securing a major donor gift tends to be a long-term process – typically 18 months or more – which makes milestone evidence particularly important both to keep you on track and to give you positive encouragement. The mental metrics will help you to orientate your behaviour for influence results.

Step 3: Consider the context

The context can make a significant difference to the outcome. Think about where, when and with whom you will achieve it. This links to Tool 13: Try philanthropic pre-suasion – prime for success, introduced in Chapter 4. When you're considering the context, it's important you take into account the donor's point of view as well as your own.

Taking each element:

- *Where?* Where should this outcome happen? Where would be a good place for you and where not? And for the prospect? Is there an ideal setting for you? And for them? What can you do to create that ideal setting?

- *When?* Is this an outcome for the next few weeks, the next few months or for years ahead? Do you have a deadline you have to meet? What would be a good timeframe from your point of view? To what time-frame is the prospect working?

- *With whom?* Who else should be there to help make the outcome possible? Who would be ideal from your point of view? Who would be ideal from the prospect's point of view? (This also connects to the resources question below.)

When considering the prospect's needs and interests, think specifically about:

- *Their hygiene factors and motivations.* (See Tool 3: Create a philanthropic PIN code.) What reassurances (hygiene factors) might you have to give them before they will consider making the gift?

- *What is their LIM-it?* (See Tool 10: Set out your LIM-its.) You may not know exactly their range of possible outcomes – Like, Intend and Must – but it's useful to consider what they might be as a way to access the prospect's perceptions and concerns.

Step 4: Establish your resources

You will either have resources available – people or things – or you'll need to find some. Make a list of the current resources to which you have access. When doing this, consider:

- *People.* Who can help – colleagues, friends, other donors, senior volunteers? Are there role models you can turn to for advice, ideas or even inspiration?

- *Collateral.* What collateral would help – a brochure, a leave-behind document, a model of the project, case studies or reports on previous successes, a video?

Finally, be clear about what resources you *don't* have access to and therefore cannot control. For example, if you can't produce a beautiful, slick TV-quality DVD of a project, what resources do you have that would help create the sense of wonder you believe the project engenders? A series of photographs? Testimonies or quotes from users?

Step 5: Consider the consequences

There may be wider issues arising from any outcome that you want. We call this the *ecology of the outcome.* By 'ecology' we mean:

- The extent to which the outcome fits with your, your organisation's and the prospect's values and beliefs. Ideally, no one should feel disappointed or uncomfortable.

- The likelihood of any outcome encouraging a long-term relationship. A gift achieved at the expense of the prospect feeling manipulated is likely to scupper any future relationship.

For instance, you get a grant from an alcohol company that helps secure your financial result, but alienates other key prospects who disagree with the ethics of taking money from such a company. A short-term win results in long-term loss.

When considering the ecology of an outcome, it is useful to ask two key questions:

1. What are the short- and long-term advantages of committing to this outcome – for me, my organisation and our beneficiaries?

2. What are the potential disadvantages of committing to this outcome – for me, my organisation, and for others?

Even when you're sure you're behaving ethically, there can be conflicts with values, either for you personally or for your organisation.

- *Personal uncertainty.* In this case, you may feel uncomfortable. For example, is this older person vulnerable when you speak to them about their gift? By reading this book, you have access to a range of psychological techniques. Are you using them to help communicate your message more clearly, or are you being manipulative? Alternatively, a prospect may have the means and inclination to help your cause, but you may dislike their sexist attitude. How much sexism are you prepared to put up with? (And are they really sexist? Or is it that they're from an older generation/different culture and unthinking in talking the way they do?)

• *Organisational uncertainty.* Some organisational values might also impact the way you go about raising money. For example, two leading UK charities disagree fundamentally on the propriety of a particular technique to secure legacy/bequest pledges. One is happy to organise events in care homes for elders, where residents approach their peers and ask whether they would consider pledging a bequest. Another refuses to use this technique, believing it to be unethical. Who's right?

Step 6: Anticipate challenges

There's a universal truth: 'Anything that can go wrong will go wrong.' Consequently, you need to prepare for all the things that could go wrong and that would stop you achieving your well-formed outcome.

Below are some examples of things you can expect to go awry as you tread a path towards your result. All have a basis in harsh personal experience!

• How will you cope if you or the prospect is late, and instead of having 45 minutes for the 'pitch' or meeting you have just 20?

- What will you do if your iPad or other technology doesn't work and your beautiful PowerPoint presentation won't load?

- How will you recover if you make some social gaffe – for example, forget someone's name or provide a buffet with food that someone can't eat for dietary or religious reasons?

- What will you do if the answer is 'no' to your proposition? (We have a whole section that helps with this: Tool 20: Manage the nine fundraising 'no's).

Step 7: Take the first step

Finally, you need to follow the advice of Chinese philosopher Lao Tze and begin the longest journey with a single step. Or if you like your advice more twenty-first century, take Nike's advice and 'Just Do It'. We often procrastinate about difficult things, and the reality is that you can never collect enough information about the prospect or prepare for every eventuality. The desire to do so can often lead to endless delay – especially if you are nervous.

The key is to start. Begin to draft the email, to dial the number, to set up the meeting. As soon as you've done that, you'll find that your preparation skills kick in.

Tool 10:
Set out your LIM-its

When to use it: If you need to establish a number of possible outcomes with varying degrees of acceptability, then Like, Intend and Must is a terrific way to lay out options.

Practice grade: 2

It's sometimes difficult to know whether a prospect's potential is, say, £250,000 or £2 million. So how do you avoid setting a specific financial goal that is meaningless? How do you make it challenging but possible? We use a technique called the LIM-it, adapted from an idea by the late great academic and consultant Gavin Kennedy.[2] This is especially useful when you're negotiating a company sponsorship, but it can be applied to many fundraising situations.

LIM stands for Like, Intend and Must, and the '-it' encourages you to think of maximums and minimums (Limit). Here are some examples from a fundraiser working for a theatre that's looking to secure support from HNWI and companies.

---

[2] Gavin Kennedy, *Everything is Negotiable* (2008).

- *Like:* what you ideally want – a £5 million one-off gift from the philanthropist or a three-year £100,000 sponsorship deal from the business.

- *Intend:* what you can accept – an individual gift of £2–3 million from the philanthropist or a two-year £50,000 sponsorship deal from the business.

- *Must:* the minimum you need or can accept, and if you don't get it, it's no deal – maybe a gift of £5 million for the studio naming rights, or £25,000 sponsorship for a specific project from the business.

The LIM-it technique is useful in that it forces you to think in terms of a range of possible solutions, and that then allows you to be specific and flexible. There are a number of different ways to calculate your LIM-it, but the most important elements are to:

- Set what you'd Like to get at a level that means your fundraising needs are reflected in the best possible outcome.

- Frame what you Intend to get as something that you believe might meet the interests of both parties.

- Be confident in what you Must get so that if for any reason that outcome is not achievable you know to walk away.

You can think about it visually (Figure 3.2).

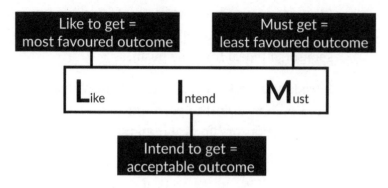

Figure 3.2: Working out your LIM-it

Importantly, you can also consider this from both parties' point of view – yours and the prospect's (Figure 3.3).

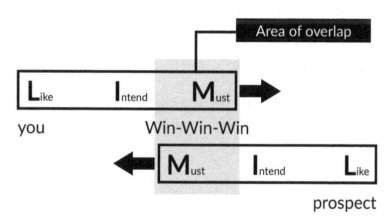

Figure 3.3: The LIM-it model from both parties' perspectives

You can see how the area of overlap can lead to a win-win-win – that is, a win for you, a win for the prospect and a win for the beneficiaries or organisation. Everyone needs to win. And it's important the prospect doesn't subsequently feel they were 'talked into' a gift. Make sure you leave them feeling positive about their choice.

Understanding the LIM–its of the corporate mind

Let's look at how this tool might work when trying to conclude a corporate sponsorship between a charity and a business.

LifeRace is a fictional cancer charity seeking support for its Women's Breast Cancer Run from the insurance company Driverco (also fictional). Driverco only insures women drivers.

LifeRace's event is obviously socially worthwhile and the target market – women – makes sense from Driverco's point of view. So Driverco offers the charity a modest, philanthropic-style corporate social responsibility (CSR) investment. But Blanca, LifeRace's Head of Corporate Affairs, came from the private sector herself. She's well aware that Driverco could potentially gain a significant commercial benefit from its association with the cause, far in excess of what it's offering under CSR.

Blanca calculates LifeRace could provide a number of straight marketing opportunities for Driverco. These range from name exposure – branding on runners' t-shirts, banners near the start and finish lines, logo on posters, etc. – to allowing the company to provide a goodie bag to every woman taking part, including information on its insurance services. For Blanca, these possibilities mean she should have a LIM-it of commercial payoffs.

She prepares her LIM-its across three different kinds of support (Table 3.3).

Table 3.3: LIM-its for Driverco

	Like	Intend	Must
Cash investment	£100,000 upfront	£75,000 upfront	£50,000 upfront
	10% of the value of any policy sold to participants	5% of the value of any policy sold	£10 for every policy sold
Marketing support	Driverco to pay for race signage and t-shirts	Driverco to pay for race signage	Driverco to pay for the t-shirts
In-kind support	Driverco to provide 100 race stewards from staff volunteers	Driverco to pay for lunch for any volunteers	Driverco to email staff about volunteering

Blanca goes into the meeting with Driverco with her Like, Intend, Must thought out. She gets her Like in cash investment and marketing support, and her Intend for in-kind support. Driverco is happy it's getting a good investment, and Blanca is happy with the level of support. It's a win-win-win.

There are three key advantages to the LIM-it approach:

- It forces you to be specific about the range of options you want. Maybe the most important are the Like and Must – *Like* encourages ambition. *Must* forces you to value your proposition.

- It keeps you on track about what you want and whether you're getting it – or whether you need to/ should change or adapt it.

- When you're skilled in using the tool, you can – as Blanca does – swap between the elements to create a 'pick'n'mix' outcome that meets a range of needs.

The LIM-it framework is most powerful when you also use it to establish the prospect's Like, Intend and Must. Going back to the LifeRace example, Blanca would need to think through Driverco's LIM-it. Would Driverco Like sole branding/ awareness opportunities and be prepared to pay more for these? Is the goodie bag with the company's information the most important element for Driverco or simply an element they Intend to secure? Are the volunteering opportunities a Must because it's part of their staff retention strategy... or simply a Like element they want to add on? It's not always easy to work out someone else's LIM-it, but it's worth having a go as a way of shaping your preparation. You should also pay attention in conversations for clues about the prospect's LIM.

LIM-its are clearly very useful in a negotiation-type corporate fundraising situation, but you can also use them to great effect with individual prospects in a more philanthropic context.

The LIM-it framework helps you to identify what you and the prospect want. But the prospect may still have a challenge with the way you present your ideas. This is where the next tool, flexible framing or reframing, comes in.

Tool 11:
Flexibly reframe

When to use it: Reframing is useful to take the same basic idea or proposition and present it in a different or more appealing way.

Practice grade: 3

Reframing or flexible framing is choosing to present your idea or issue in a different way to make it more appealing to the potential prospect. There are, of course, a number of techniques within the general tool. Figure 3.4 illustrates an example of information presented in a particular frame. Can you answer the question? Look at the footnote to check whether you got it right. Or if you're stuck.[3]

---

[3] If you were trying to solve this in some clever mathematical way, stop now. The answer is to turn the image upside down. The answer then is clear and simple – 87. The point is that we sometimes try to solve a problem in only one frame, when reframing the problem would make the solution much clearer.

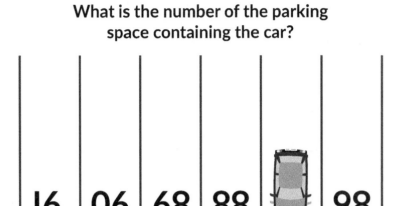

Figure 3.4: Reframing

Mental decision-making software: Metaprograms

A reframe can be as simple as changing the way you describe the same information to attract a different audience. Most fundraisers seek 'a gift or donation'. But there are some prospects who don't like to think of what they're doing as a giveaway, but rather as a social investment. Sites like kiva.org and lendwithcare.org are specifically designed to appeal to such individuals. They talk exclusively about investments and loans. The reality is that most of these 'investors' will never ask for their money back, but (social) investment fits better with their mental model of wanting to help people to help themselves through business.

In another piece of flexible framing, charitywater.org makes a very bold claim that, 'Every penny [you donate] goes to the field' and nothing to overheads – such as office rent, salaries, fundraising costs, etc. Now in fact all they have done is to raise money separately from a second group of donors and created a restricted fund that pays salaries, rent, communications costs and so on. In practice, many charities could do that by asking some donors to agree to meet the 'overhead costs'. It's actually just a piece of accounting, since every charity of any size must have overhead or core costs to carry out their work. BUT framing the proposition as 'All your money goes to the field' is very powerful.

Reframing is a technique often used to test out attitudes in opinion surveys. In one such example, Americans think their country spends too much on 'welfare' by a factor of almost two to one.[4] In the same survey more than two-thirds think it doesn't spend enough on 'assistance to the poor'. There could technically be a difference between these two phrases, but the respondents weren't asked about any distinction – they were simply responding to the framing and reframing. However, the language reframe clearly makes a significant difference to the answers.

 Top tip: Innovators often reframe

Reframing isn't new. In the eighteenth century, James Watt needed investors to help finance him to improve his engine to make it commercially viable. So that the investors would understand the power of his machine, he invented the term 'horsepower' rather than talking about what was actually pressure per square inch.

---

[4] https://scholars.org/contribution/what-americans-think-about-poverty-and-how-reduce-it

Steve Jobs of Apple did something similar when he launched the iPod. He didn't explain the capacity in gigabits or compare it to any of the other competitor MP3 players available. Instead, he reframed the iPod storage device as a '1,000 songs in your pocket'.

Consider how you could reframe your proposition to make it attractive and impactful.

Being able to reframe – or flexibly frame – your fundraising case is essential to widening your reach. Think of it as like sending computer files in compatible formats. If you want to send an Excel spreadsheet, the person at the other end also needs to have Excel or a compatible piece of software to open it. In fundraising, you need to work out what mental software your prospect has and package your data – words and ideas – in their format. These precise pieces of mental software are called metaprograms. Put simply, they are more specific preferences or habits in thinking. The way someone speaks gives an excellent insight into which of these programs they are using to make a decision or process an experience.

Being skilled in identifying and using metaprograms is very useful when you want to:

- frame your proposition in ways that appeal very explicitly to a particular individual

- discover why someone isn't responding to your proposition in the way you thought they would.

A number of different metaprograms have been identified by psychologists. Each offers insights into different ways of thinking that individuals have. There are probably just five that are really useful in fundraising: match/mismatch; associated/disassociated; towards/away from; big chunk/small chunk; and past, present, future.

In each case, your preference may be the same as or different from that of your prospect. It is important that you don't assume anything but rather build your approach on observed behaviours. That way, you are much more likely to succeed in winning them over.

Let's look at a couple of them in a little more detail.

Match/mismatch

Look at the image in Figure 3.5. Take a minute to think about it, then describe the relationship of the objects.

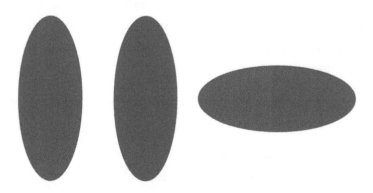

Figure 3.5: Match/mismatch

How did you describe that relationship?

- 'There are three ovals, all apparently the same size, and one is over on its side.'

- 'There's an oval on its side and then two others upright. They might be the same size.'

- 'There are two upright ovals, and one oval that has fallen over on its side out of the set.'

- 'There are three objects – one on its side right over to the right, one next to it in the middle upright, and then another one further away also upright.'

Notice at least one of these descriptions seems like the most obvious one to you, while others you would never have dreamed of saying – they seem just too 'odd'. That's because some people initially sort for difference (mismatch) and some people sort for sameness (match). And some people sort first for sameness and then for difference.

Let's try another example. Take a look at the room you're in. If you're in your office, compare it with your favourite room at home. If you're at home, compare it with your office. When you make the comparison, do you:

- predominantly think about things that are *the same*? (It's also very simply furnished; it's got photos of my family like the house; and it's a mess like the sitting room)

- predominantly think about things that are *different*? (Here is so hi tech – I love the simplicity of my uncluttered home; I've got photos of my family at home – here it's charts and graphs; the office is tidy, thank goodness – unlike the sitting room).

How can the fact that some people look for similarities and others for difference – match or mismatch – be useful in major gift fundraising? Think about the response you might get to your fundraising proposal. 'Thank you for explaining your case about your work on international development. But I wonder how you're really different from Oxfam? I need to see some extra value to make it worth my while contributing to you specifically.' A question such as this is a clue that this mismatcher needs some difference data before they will say yes. Equally a question like, 'This is all very interesting. But I'm keen to support a range of causes committed to international development. How do you complement Oxfam?' is a clue to a matching preference. In that case, look for similarities to share.

Obviously it's better to know your prospect's preference before you begin the 'business' part of the discussion. And to that end, it's worth having some standard cueing questions/situations to elicit or establish their preference. For example, try asking:

- How do you like this location compared to where we met last time? ('It's about the same distance from home.' (match) 'It's a much more business-like venue for the discussion.' (mismatch))

- How does lunch compare to last time? ('Looks like they have the same kind of menu – a mix of salads and more substantial dishes.' (match) 'The service was much slower and less friendly.' (mismatch))

Associated/disassociated

A second very common and useful metaprogram is associated/disassociated.

To help make the distinction here, think about a genuine conversation you had recently that was difficult or distressing. Take the time to recall it in as much detail as you can. Notice how you communicate the experience to yourself. What comes first – the challenging image, the harsh words that were said, the feelings of anger and frustration?

Now notice how you accessed the memory. As it came to you, did you shut your eyes or defocus and replay the situation as if through your own eyes and ears, or did you keep your eyes open and recall the event as an external observer, hearing yourself speak, seeing yourself in that situation?

Here the distinction is between:

*   associated – in your own body through your own perception

*   disassociated – observing or noticing yourself from outside your own body.

Some people associate very easily. They can recall situations from their childhood incredibly strongly and can 'flash back' to the feelings, sights, sounds and even smells from their early life as if they were there now. (If they're doing this, they're probably producing a lot of oxytocin, too.) Some do this so strongly that they can even 'associate' as other people. When you say:

Imagine you're a 10-year-old girl in northern Uganda obliged to walk 6 miles twice a day for water. It's only 7am but you feel tired in the heat because although you've already walked 3 miles, you still have as far to go again.

You'll have some of your audience visibly wilting as they step into the body of the girl – or what they imagine that girl to be – and experience the walk.

Others will find it hard to 'be' the girl in any way. To them you say:

Think about a television documentary about the challenges of growing up in a rural community in the developing world. It tells you about a young girl – maybe just 10 years old – and it shows her walking to collect water from the well in the next village. What do you feel as you watch the little girl on the TV screen? If you were there, wouldn't you want to help that little girl carry the heavy buckets? Or say something to encourage her?

For these people, the preference is to respond through disassociation.

Noticing this distinction can be important. Our experience suggests that although many fundraisers find it easy to associate, the same is not true of all prospects – which is possibly why some prospects don't identify emotionally with the cause in the intense way you do. If you're aware your prospect prefers to be disassociated, you need to reframe the proposition to meet their needs. Make sure you explore

Tool 17: Pivot perceptual positions – choose another angle in Chapter 5.

Towards/away from

Think about a personal goal you have – maybe to do with your weight or fitness, or maybe a relationship. Notice that you either thought first about:

- a positive situation you wanted to get into – to look great on the beach, or to have a really happy holiday

or

- a negative situation you wanted to get out of – to lose weight, to stop having rows and feeling stressed.

Again, these two approaches represent two different kinds of thinking – moving towards and away from. As with the other metaprograms, recognising these preferences should encourage you to adapt your fundraising communication with the prospect. Classically, it's about deciding whether you should present your proposal in terms of moving towards a solution or away from a bad situation. For example:

'Your gift to our hospice will ensure cancer sufferers can avoid the pain and indignity of dying alone at home or impersonal care in the hospital.' (away from)

or

'Your gift will help us create a positive and holistic haven where we can support our cancer patients as they move towards a peaceful death.' (towards)

Just as you probably prefer one of the statements over the other, so too will your different prospects. As before, use questions early in the solicitation meeting or telephone call to cue you about which of these preferences is most evident in the prospect. If you know they've just had some change in their lives – new job, new house, that kind of thing – find a way of asking them why they chose that change. They'll most likely respond in a towards or away from style: 'I wanted to get away from that neighbourhood' or 'I wanted to come somewhere warmer like here'. Once you know their preference, you're in a better position to frame your ask in the way that's most effective for that person. Again, notice the links here to the *gains or losses* options we discussed in Tool 5: Build an =mc story arc in Chapter 2.

Big chunk/small chunk

People process ideas at different levels. A very useful technique to help you connect with them and influence a person's ideas when trying to win them over is to do what's called 'chunking up' and 'chunking down'. To illustrate how chunking works, think of a plane:

- To chunk up, think of categories like 'kinds of transport'. To chunk up more, think of 'travel'.

- To chunk down, think of 'big planes'. To chunk down further, think of a specific plane – a Boeing 747.

Big chunk/small chunk is a useful metaprogram not only to help you get on your prospect's wavelength, but also to help pitch your idea at the right level.

For prospects who prefer big chunk, you might develop a proposition that tells them:

> The situation for people with HIV/AIDS in sub-Saharan Africa is appalling. As a society we need to address this issue.

A slightly smaller chunk might be:

> In Zimbabwe, there is simply not enough medical aid available for the 15 million people with HIV/AIDS. As residents of a developed and wealthy country like the UK, we have a duty to help them.

Small chunk:

> Abotho is a town in Northern Zimbabwe where almost 10,000 people are HIV positive. That's a population the size of our community here in Smallville. We need to connect to that community and support them.

And an even smaller chunk:

> In Abotho I met Lasha who was infected with HIV by her husband. She now has full-blown AIDS. Lasha can't look after her children aged five and seven without medication. But medication costs $25 a month. Lasha – when she can work – earns just $250 in a year. Your gift of $1000 will not only pay for the life-saving treatment she needs for the foreseeable future, it will also buy her the food that will help to keep her healthy, and it will pay for her children's education. They, at least, will have a better start in life.

Notice that small chunk doesn't mean a small or individual-ised gift. You could finish up the last ask with: 'And if you can gift £10,000 we can bulk-buy the medication and you could help 20 women like Lasha to have a future.'

Chunking up is very useful when you're trying to find common ground, and chunking down when you want to get to a specific arrangement. Going either way is relatively easy to do with practice and good questions.

To chunk up, try these questions:

- What will this give us/you?

- What purpose will be served by doing that?

- What's your intention with that specific request or action?

- What general principles or values can we agree on?

- What general situation or cluster is this an example of?

To chunk down, try these questions:

- With what specific results?

- What are examples of this concern or advantage?

- What specifically is the challenge or agreement?

- What would be a preference between one or more possibilities?

- Give me some detail or an example of this.

Powerful propositions: Learning from Leonardo

Your proposition probably needs to be underpinned by the hygiene factors of spreadsheets, PowerPoints, Gantt charts and so on to give it logical credibility. But logic isn't everything. To make your case as strong as possible, you need to play to your strengths but frame or reframe them around the needs or concerns of the prospect. The following is a brilliant example. It's a real letter written by Leonardo da Vinci in 1483, seeking employment with the Duke of Milan. It lists 10 reasons why the Duke should hire him – detailing his skills and talents, but presenting them in terms of meeting the military challenges the Duke might face. Notice that da Vinci only mentions the thing he really wants to do – make art – after his proposition list of 10 reasons. And even here he suggests his talent can help make the Duke and his father look good. Everything is targeted at the Duke and his interests. Plus he offers a free trial! It's worth a careful read.

> Having, most illustrious lord, seen and considered the experiments of all those who pose as masters in the art of inventing instruments of war, and finding that their inventions differ in no way from

those in common use, I am emboldened, without prejudice to anyone, to solicit an appointment of acquainting your Excellency with certain of my secrets.

1. I can construct bridges which are very light and strong and very portable, with which to pursue and defeat the enemy; and others more solid, which resist fire or assault, yet are easily removed and placed in position; and I can also burn and destroy those of the enemy.

2. In case of a siege I can cut off water from the trenches and make pontoons and scaling ladders and other similar contrivances.

3. If by reason of the elevation or the strength of its position a place cannot be bombarded, I can demolish every fortress if its foundations have not been set on stone.

4. I can also make a kind of cannon which is light and easy of transport, with which to hurl small stones like hail, and of which the smoke causes great terror to the enemy, so that they suffer heavy loss and confusion.

5. I can noiselessly construct to any prescribed point subterranean passages either straight or winding, passing if necessary underneath trenches or a river.

6. I can make armoured wagons carrying artillery, which shall break through the most serried

ranks of the enemy, and so open a safe passage for his infantry.

7. If occasion should arise, I can construct cannon and mortars and light ordnance in shape both ornamental and useful and different from those in common use.

8. When it is impossible to use cannon I can supply in their stead catapults, mangonels, trabocchi, and other instruments of admirable efficiency not in general use – in short, as the occasion requires I can supply infinite means of attack and defence.

9. And if the fight should take place upon the sea I can construct many engines most suitable either for attack or defence and ships which can resist the fire of the heaviest cannon, and powders or weapons.

10. In time of peace, I believe that I can give you as complete satisfaction as anyone else in the construction of buildings both public and private, and in conducting water from one place to another.

I can further execute sculpture in marble, bronze or clay, also in painting I can do as much as anyone else, whoever he may be.

Moreover, I would undertake the commission of the bronze horse, which shall endure with immortal glory and eternal honour the auspicious memory of your father and of the illustrious house of Sforza.

And if any of the aforesaid things should seem to anyone impossible or impracticable, I offer myself as ready to make trial of them in your park or in whatever place shall please your Excellency, to whom I commend myself with all possible humility.

Leonardo da Vinci

(By the way, da Vinci got a job with the Duke and kept it for 16 years, until the French invaded the city and captured his employer.)[5]

Framing and reframing are hugely helpful to shape and organise your thinking. Our final tool in this chapter will help you consider the key elements of your proposition in sequence.

---

[5] From I.A. Richter (ed.), *Selections from the Notebooks of Leonardo da Vinci* (1952), pp. 275–77.

Tool 12:
Link think, feel, do

When to use it: This is a must-use tool, ideal when you only have a few minutes to share your idea or at the end of an interaction as a mental leave-behind. You summarise, in a powerful sequence, your key message combining a fact, an emotion and an action.

Practice grade: 3

To sell an idea effectively, you need to be able to summarise it in a powerful and simple way. One way is to organise it through three elements – think, feel, do (Figure 3.6).

- *Think.* What will people think, know or understand in your proposition? This could relate to the facts or data. It could be positive – the tangible benefits to users; the payoffs from the new project; the opportunities it offers. Or it could be negative – the scale of the problem; the number of people impacted; the amount of damage done.

- *Feel.* How do you want the prospect to feel about your proposition? What emotion – pride, happiness, excitement, a sense of relief – do you want to generate? Again, it could be the negative versions: shame, anger, sadness. Identifying the correct emotion, and one that is strong enough, is super important.

- *Do.* What action would you like the prospect to take to move things on? How can they specifically contribute? If it's money you're after, are you looking for a gift immediately or a longer-term relationship? And if it's too early in the relationship to ask for money, is the action round committing to a next meeting?

Think	**Feel**	**Do**

What do you want people to think, know or understand?	**What do you want people to feel or respond emotionally?**	**What specific action do you want people to take?**

Figure 3.6: Think, feel, do

 ## The unanswered phone... a think, feel, do

We spent many years working as consultants with the UK's National Society for the Prevention of Cruelty to Children (NSPCC).

After the NSPCC merged with Childline, the telephone advice helpline, the first priority was to raise funds for the service, which was sadly missing targets to respond to urgent calls from children and young people at risk. There was an urgent need to organise an event for a number of HNWI prospects and ask them for financial support.

Here's a simplified summary of the proposition we helped a senior fundraiser develop using the think, feel, do framework.

Think	Feel	Do
'We've not been able to answer all calls to the helpline. Without enough trained volunteers, there are times we're missing one in four calls.' 'Many children aren't able to stay on the line for as long as it takes to be answered. They often only have a few rings to get through. We want to be sure that every child who needs to contact us can always do so, 24/7.'	'I'm horrified that we can't deliver the vital service children deserve. I guess you are too.' 'I lie awake at night wondering what any of those missed calls might mean. My guess is you might be very concerned too. I want to feel proud of the service we provide. And I want you to feel sure that children and young people can trust us to answer their calls.'	'We need to introduce new working practices to ensure that we answer all calls in time. We need to update out technology. We need to recruit and train more volunteers. It all costs money.' 'With your gift, you can make sure that each and every call is answered in a timely way, and the child on the other end of the call can be helped.'

You can see how the three key elements work together. The 'one in four' fact is designed to make the prospects concerned.

If you can, go further. Make your message imaginative – like the example of Bill Gates and the mosquitoes mentioned in Chapter 2. What can you do to share your vision in an unusual way? How will you make it engaging/visceral? Here's a piece of fundraising theatre we designed for an event for a helpline charity with around 200 high-value donors present.

The prospects were in an auditorium, facing a stage. On the stage we arranged for four phones to be on four tables, with a person sitting beside three of them. The stage was in darkness. All four phones began to ring. Phone 1 was lit up and quickly answered. And then phone 2. And then phone 3. But the fourth phone was not answered. It continued to ring for an almost unbearable 90 seconds. (That's a long time!)

The fundraiser came forward to speak as the last phone stopped and was replaced by the sound of a call being hung up. All the phones went back into darkness. The message was clear and powerful. We need your help to answer that fourth call.

How could you make your appeal feel as real as this? We've included some examples we've been involved with below.

Get physical – use your imagination

We've helped organisations to develop a wide range of imaginative ways to prepare to deliver their think, feel, do proposition – often involving a physical example.

A4 paper and chicken

The brilliant CEO of Compassion in World Farming, Philip Lymbery, constructed a terrific way to share the impact of the limited space factory chickens have to live in before being slaughtered. He would take out a piece of A4 paper and fold it in half to A5. He'd explain to the audience that A5 was the space a caged chicken had to live in when Compassion in World Farming was founded. And 40 years later, after campaigning and legislation, the amount of space available for a chicken was... A4. He paused, then opened up the sheet of paper. He concluded:

> If you think that that A4 space is enough for a humane animal life, then our work is done, and we don't need your support. If you are shocked at how little space that is... then please recommit to helping is to do much, much more.

Drinking straw and asthma

Asthma UK used a straw to demonstrate to its audience what it was like to have breathing difficulties. They explained that having asthma made it twice as hard to breathe. They then gave a straw to everyone at a fundraising meeting and asked them to breathe through it – and keep breathing through it – for a minute. (Try it yourself – it's really hard.) The breathing fact, combined with the scary feeling engendered by using the straw, paved the way to making the ask.

More than any description in words, this brought home to the audience the frightening effect of asthma and related breathing illnesses. And it opened the way to persuading the audience to support medical research into cures and treatments.

Art gallery and screws

Modern Art Oxford (formerly the Museum of Modern Art) sent out a direct mail package to potential local commercial sponsors. It consisted of a very large screw with some picture wire, attached to a piece of card. Inside was a note explaining they couldn't use the screw or the wire without having pictures to hang on the walls of the gallery – could the sponsor help? The package was a fun and imaginative way to bring home the fact that they needed money to support the purchase of contemporary art. And that companies could feel good and gain publicity by supporting the purchase. The alternative was an empty gallery. How would the sponsor feel about that?

 Action summary

An essential part of getting your ask ready is to use one or more of the key tools in the preparation stage to properly shape your own thinking, and to consider how you might present your ideas to address both your interests and those of your prospect or prospects.

✓ Begin by being clear about what you want or need. Develop a concrete *well-formed outcome* to guide your action and your choice of tools.

✓ As the Rolling Stones say, 'You can't always get what you want' – therefore you need to map out a range of possible and acceptable results. To do this, establish your *LIM-it* – your best, acceptable and least favoured options. And consider what the LIM-it of your prospect is.

✓ Consider how to change the way your proposition is received using *flexible frames*. There are a number of metaprogrammes that you can change to fit your prospect's way of thinking.

✓ Summarise your approach using the think, feel, do framework so you end up with a simple clear message. Think of a way to share this summary message imaginatively.

Chapter 4

Persuasion

The only way on earth to influence other people is to talk about what they want and show them how to get it.

Dale Carnegie

Having spent the first three Ps getting ready, it's time to move into direct interpersonal engagement. Most of what we cover in this chapter is focused on face-to-face meetings – or one-to-one Zoom calls. It is always best to make an ask in person, but you can also apply many of the tools and ideas to written communications such as emails and to phone calls.

In this chapter, focused on *Persuasion*, we focus on four tools that ensure you can work with anyone, no matter how different to you or how challenging the interaction. These are:

- Plan your pre-suasion through *philanthropic priming*.

- Use *listen/silence* to ensure you are engaged with your prospect.

- Build *rapid rapport* to get and stay on their wavelength.

- Adapt your *language style* to match the prospect's preferences.

Figure 4.1: The persuasion power tools

Tool 13:
Try philanthropic pre-suasion – prime for success

When to use it: Just before you make the ask – prospects can be encouraged by subtle cues delivered early on before you actually make the ask.

Practice Grade: 3

We mentioned pre-suasion, or priming, earlier. They are broadly the same thing, and we'll use the terms interchangeably. Essentially, priming involves creating a psychological readiness in the prospect for your key message. This can be so subtle that the prospect will scarcely notice it. More than many of the other techniques in the book, when you use pre-suasion you must be careful to use it ethically.

One of our favourite works on priming comes from Robert Cialdini, Emeritus Professor of Marketing and Psychology at Arizona State University. In his latest book, *Pre-suasion,*[1] he explores many of the key ideas, complementing the research done by Daniel Kahneman and others.

---

[1] Robert Cialdini, *Pre-suasion: A Revolutionary Way to Influence and Persuade* (2016).

Cialdini describes an experiment in France. A number of middle-aged men are approached over a period of time by a young woman in the street and asked for directions to a specific address. The men help where they can and are thanked. It's important to say that the woman is attractive – but there is no hint of any inappropriate engagement. This is the initial priming – to make the subjects feel helpful.

A hundred metres further on, the same man is stopped by a second woman, also attractive. She tells him that her mobile phone has been stolen by four tough-looking youths standing nearby. She asks the man to approach them and request they return her phone. (All of the participants, apart from the man, are of course involved in the social experiment, so there is no actual risk.) Not surprisingly, some 80% of the men stopped say 'no'. What's amazing is that, faced with this very challenging request, 20% of men approached say 'yes' and do indeed approach the youths to ask them to return the phone. The experiment was repeated a number of times to produce a robust sample. The story gets more interesting when we look at slightly different priming.

In a second sample, 37% of the men approached – almost twice as many – said 'yes' to the same request. The difference the second time around was that in the first priming experiment the men were asked for directions to Martin Street – a pretty anonymous name. In the second run the men were asked by the woman to help find Valentine's Street. Using this and a number of other related examples, Cialdini explains that the mention of the word 'Valentine' brought to mind the idea of romance and romantic gestures. This priming outweighed any potential danger to more of the men being asked to intervene.[2] And it's not only men this affects. A similar experiment was carried out with women as the subjects and the results were the same.

What's the learning here?

- One is that attractive people, regardless of gender or sexuality, tend to do well in situations when asking for a favour – or a gift. (You probably knew that from life.)

- A second wider learning is that by giving people a subtle psychological cue about a mindset or thought, you can help produce a result more in line with the outcome that you want.

- Let's repeat the key message here. Priming or pre-suasion needs to be subtle. And it generally needs to happen when the prospect is thinking about something else.

---

[2] When asked, the percentage of men who noticed the priming cue was precisely zero. The implication is that people aren't paying attention – which is why priming is so effective – and so dangerous in the wrong hands.

There are loads of other priming examples from business and charity. Here are just a few:

- Customers will buy more French wine in a super-market if there is French-sounding music playing in the wine section. The same is true of German wine when there is German-sounding music playing. Most people won't notice the music cue, but they will respond to it.

- People will respond to the cue of reciprocity. Cialdini describes as a universal principal that if I help you, you'll tend to help me. (Think of receiving a present from someone at Christmas when you haven't bought one for them. You've broken a key human interaction principle and feel guilty.) In McDonald's, customers were given a balloon for their children either on the way in or on the way out. Parents given the balloon on the way in bought 25% more in their children's happy meals. And twice as much coffee for them-selves. The upfront gift pre-suaded them to respond.

- When we delivered a presentation at a 2000+ people conference in Washington DC, we asked ushers to give out leaflets with information about the book *Change for Good*. The bags they used when handing out the leaflets had a lion image on them. As people entered the room, we played music – some from *The Lion King* film. One of us mentioned in the presenta-tion we had recently been on a trip to Lyon in France. Then at one point in the middle of some other ques-tions, we asked everyone to write down the name of a creature that lives in the jungle. Some 90% of the audience immediately wrote down the word 'lion' – despite the fact lions don't live in the jungle (and most of the audience knew that), and despite the fact there are lots and lots of creatures that *do* live in the jungle.[3] As with Cialdini's experiments, most people simply didn't notice the priming.

What's the implication in terms of your ask? Well, you need to think about how you could engage your prospect to put them in a receptive or philanthropic frame of mind. To do this, you could:

- Make sure you give them a warm welcome when they arrive at your premises, having provided helpful instructions to get there.

- Consider promoting reciprocity. Offer to help to make the visit easy if someone comes to your building – maybe send a map. Offer them a drink or even a snack. Ideally offer a simple gift – maybe a book about your work. Do this regardless of whether they make a gift.

- Arrange for your main reception or the room you work in to have images of others helping – ideally with their names and quotes from them.

- Tie solicitations into times and images that have a resonance for the prospect – Eid, Christmas, Hanukkah. In all the major 'Abrahamic' religions, especially, these are times when gifting and generosity

---

[3] If the same experiment is conducted without the priming, most people say 'monkey'.

are at the front of people's minds. Make use of that free priming.

- Think about the smells, sounds and sights that might help put your prospect into a more positive frame of mind about you, your organisation and your proposition. Singapore Airlines sells you an experience when you enter the plane. The stale air of a pressurised airline cabin isn't the best. Singapore recognised this and developed a custom scent worn by female cabin crew and sprayed into their hot towels.

The primed journey at UDEM

At the University of Monterrey (UDEM) in Mexico, the two individuals in charge of development in the start-up years, Beto Viesca and Isabella Navarro, brilliantly primed prospects to maximise the impact of their ask.

When the university was engaged in its first capital campaign, it was still in the process of being built. Much of the campus was little more than a building site.

Undeterred, Beto and Isabella thought about how they could use this situation to their advantage. As a prospect, you arrived at the university and parked in the car park. To walk from the car park to the board-room where the ask would be made, you followed a path where each brick had been donated by a former student, supporter or member of staff. All the bricks had simple messages (Figure 4.2) – for example, 'In honour of my inspiring lecturer Jose Antonio', or 'With thanks to my mother and father for believing in me and my education – Maria'.

Figure 4.2: Brick path at the University of Monterrey

You also passed by some amazing outdoor sculptures (Figure 4.3), designed by a famous artist, which it was explained were there as a thank you to major donors. (Donors' names were inscribed on them.) You would probably have recognised a number of the donors as your peers from Monterrey – a rich city in the north.

Figure 4.3: Outdoor sculptures at the University of Monterrey

Finally, you arrived at the main boardroom. It had a huge panoramic window overlooking the emerging campus.

As the prospect, Beto, the Development Director, would bring you to this window and show you the gaps between completed buildings. (Remember, this is partly a building site.) Specifically, he identified the space where the building to which you were going to contribute would stand. He encouraged you to mentally fill in the gap with the architect's plans you had been shown, or the model that had been brought in. You, like other prospects, would defocus as you imagined 'your' building filling that gap.

The journey from the car park was a fabulous way to prime the prospect to feel that giving was normal and that the entire campus was structured to 'reward' such gifts. The ask in the boardroom and the use of 'fillable gaps' were a stroke of genius and a great way to create a concrete imaginative engagement for the prospect.

Tool 14:
Pay absolute attention
with the silent listen

When to use it: Having had your pick of 13 tools to use, it's tempting to focus on message transmission in a range of ways. But before you do, bear in mind that there is significant power in being silent so that you can *listen*. Use this tool when you're looking for a response.

Practice grade: 3

An outstanding communicator will commit completely to paying attention to the person from whom they are seeking support. Developing this ability will add significantly to your effectiveness in making the ask. We're combining two techniques here, which by chance are not just complementary but also anagrams of each other – silent and listen.

Silent

This is about the importance of creating space for the prospect to process their thoughts, take in the information you have given them and formulate a response. With more space, they will speak and share their opinions and views.

Remaining silent is one of the most powerful tools available to the fundraiser. It is very tempting to keep talking and 'selling', but that's a mistake. You should pause regularly as you share ideas and information and check for a response. Always *pause* – stay silent – immediately after you make the ask. Wait for them to make the next move… no matter how long it takes. If you have the courage or patience to do this, the prospect will almost always fill the gap with a useful response. Wait for that response, then make a judgement about what it means – and how you should progress.

Listen

Use the space that your silence offers to listen very carefully – to pay exceptional attention to what the prospect is saying and what they're not saying. By focusing on listening, and showing very clearly you are listening, you make the other person feel that they and their opinion are valued. Listening is not just using your ears. It's also noticing body language and more. The Chinese, with their centuries of wisdom, are already on to this.

You may be aware that Chinese ideograms often combine a number of symbols to create a single word or phrase. This makes Chinese an exceptionally rich language. One of the most interesting elements in this context is the cluster of symbols linked together to represent listening (Figure 4.4). If, like us, you don't speak Chinese, the listening symbol is made up of six other ideographic components. These are: You, Eyes, Undivided Attention, Heart, King and Ear.

Figure 4.4: The Chinese symbol for 'listening'

As you can see, this impressive combination goes way beyond what is commonly described as active listening in English.

Let's explore each of these components:

- *You* – focus your energy on the act of listening. Make sure you're not listening just to prepare your answer. When someone else is talking, you need to play an active role as the listener for the communication to be effective. If you don't play your part, the rapport may be broken, or part of their message may be confused or lost.

- *Eyes* – listen with your eyes. Observe the body language and expressions of the speaker. By paying attention to what the prospect does as they talk, you will pick up so much more about how they feel about what they are saying. You'll also become more observant and interested in the prospect.

- *Undivided Attention* – give this to the speaker. Make sure you don't become distracted by anything else that's around. Distractions can come from other people when you're in a group, or even your technology. Switch off your phone! Make this person the focus of all your energy.

- *Heart* – pay attention with your heart. Don't just consider the prospect as someone capable of making a gift or investment. Be open to their opinions and their beliefs, even if they are different from yours. (Provided, of course, that they don't conflict with core values about issues such as sexism or racism.) Make sure you make the time to understand their point of view before responding.

- *King* – this is the bit we really love. The ideogram is encouraging you to treat the speaker like royalty. Imagine the prospect is the most important person in the world. This involves being courteous, of course, but it goes further: give them the respect and attention such status deserves.

- *Ear* – oddly, this is the final part of listening. Take the time to listen to the exact words and phrases being used by the prospect. (Note especially the importance of language preferences – see Tool 16: Match language style – switch sensory systems in this chapter and Tool 11: Flexibly reframe in Chapter 3.) There may be clues – words or phrasing – about what's important to them or how they feel about your proposition. And, of course, voice tone is also important in the communication, as we'll discover below.

Top tip: Stimulate to listen – use acuity questions

Good, stimulating questions will often help you find some nuggets to listen and respond to. We call these acuity questions. Acuity is the ability to closely and accurately observe how someone responds to what you do or say.

Acuity questions help you to discover more about the person or people you're meeting and how they think and make decisions. Here are some of our favourites:

- *Acuity question 1:* 'Tell me about [another cause you support]?' For example, 'I hear you're a major supporter of the contemporary art gallery. I love their exhibitions too. What first got you involved with them?' This is a great question if you're perhaps from a humanitarian agency for whom the question 'Do you think humanitarian work is important?' or 'How could we persuade you to become involved in our work?' would not be helpful. They're way too obvious and would probably lead to a cautious or even false – socially appropriate rather than truthful – answer. Instead, the idea is to find something else the prospect cares about and ask them about that. You can even do this with a subject like hobbies – for example, 'What got you into photography?' In our experience people very often talk passionately and openly about another interest they have because they don't see it as a conflict.

You're looking for an insight into their motivations and what makes them like or dislike something. Once the prospect is talking, they'll often reveal something about their philanthropic motivations – for example, in what way they appreciate how the gallery rewards them. Or even what has cheesed them off about the way they have been treated in the past by an agency to which they have given.

- *Acuity question 2:* 'How did you two meet?' This is a great question if you're meeting a couple and talking about a shared gift or investment they might make. Again, it sounds like a very natural question to ask and looks like you're simply getting to know them a bit better. But in fact the answer will provide some really useful insights into the couple's decision-making. If they say, 'You know it took us ages to get together,' that's a clue that they are quite cautious in decision-making, and will need lots of time and lots of information to make a decision about a gift. Don't push them.

  If they say, 'Well, you know, it was love at first sight – we just thought it was the right thing to do', this couple decides quickly – so maybe try some options sooner rather than later and look for whether they get excited by one or more of the ideas you put forward.

And if one person says, 'Well, he really pursued me… and eventually I said yes', you're then getting a clue that there is an unequal power dynamic – and you should prioritise convincing the more powerful partner.

- *Acuity question 3:* 'Tell me, how did you set up your business?' This is a great question when you're speaking to a businessperson. Again, it sounds very natural and looks like you're simply asking for a bit of background. In fact, the answer will provide some really useful insights into your prospect's approach to risk. Some people will be very entrepreneurial. They will say, 'I saw an opportunity and just moved for it straight away. That's the way I do business.' Another person might say, 'I looked at the market carefully and then decided to invest. It was a long-term process to build the business up.' Still another might say, 'Well, I took a lot of advice from family and various experts like my accountants and lawyer – then took action.' Whatever the answer, they're telling you something important about how they make decisions. Notice that they may well use one of the four approaches discussed on the =mc story arc: risk, crisis, opportunity and vision.

Use these acuity questions to help yourself be flexible in the way you make your ask. You can probably think of more.

What is rapport?

Sometimes you meet someone at a social event – maybe a dinner party – and spend a really enjoyable evening chatting to them, exploring shared interests, even feeling fine about disagreeing on how funny a particular TV show is. You exchange numbers and talk about meeting up in a couple of weeks.

In this interaction you've been in rapport – the process of building a connection with someone else where you and they feel on the same wavelength. Rapport is not just about agreeing on things, it's about feeling comfortable and safe to share views. This is a natural human phenomenon, and it's how we build friendships, get on with people or even just agree on shared interests.

But rapport isn't a permanent state – it can be quite transitory. When you meet up again with the person you got on with so well at the dinner party, you may find there's no connection after all. You're still the same people and share the same interests as you did two weeks before. You'd both like it to work, but the connection has just gone. The rapport has disappeared.

As a fundraiser, you need to be good at building rapport with people. This is not usually a problem with people your own age, gender and cultural background. Unfortunately – unless you are an unusual reader – people like you are a lot less likely to be in your pool of fundraising prospects. Instead, you may have to deal with people who are much older than you, who share a different value set, who are very different from you in terms of economic situation, and who even share a different faith, gender or sexuality. It's with these people that you need to be good at quickly building rapport on demand. And you need to be able to do it on the phone, writing an email, on Zoom, in a meeting or even during a cultivation event while clutching a glass of warm chardonnay in one hand and a canapé in the other.

How do you do this? You probably know someone who seems socially at ease with everyone and able to make a connection with people everywhere. This person is the sort who can charm hotel reception staff into giving them a free room upgrade, convince salespeople to offer a discount or calm down a grumpy colleague in a meeting. This person has discovered naturally the key skills and techniques to build rapport. The rest of us need to learn to do it.

Tool 15:
Build rapid rapport

When to use it: Rapid rapport is another one of our must-have tools. You probably do this naturally and unconsciously all the time. The tool we explore here is super useful when you're with someone very different from you. It is also valuable when you're worried the meeting isn't going well and you need to improve the *process* of the communication, not the *content*.

Practice grade: 4

There are a range of techniques within rapport that build on the natural processes we've already discussed. These techniques help us to build friendships and positive working relationships. Most of the time in our personal lives, we build rapport unconsciously. What we're looking at here is the ability to *consciously* build rapport – and build it fast, often under pressured situations.

Aligning your communication: Three channels

You need to understand how we send and receive information to use rapport techniques well. Let's go right back to first principles. There are three key channels we use to communicate information: words, voice and body language.

These channels are not equally important in terms of relative impact. There has been a significant amount of research done on this. The person who codified what many other scientists and social scientists from Charles Darwin to Erving Goffman also observed is Professor Albert Mehrabian of UCLA. Based on a series of careful experiments, his research in the 1980s established the relative overall impact of the three communication channels (Figure 4.5).

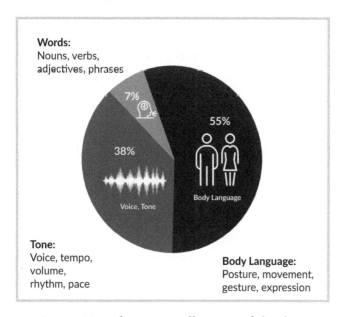

Figure 4.5: Relative overall impact of the three communication channels

Mehrabian's research is often misquoted and misunderstood, so let's be clear what the 55/38/7 ratio does and doesn't mean. Although words represent only 7% of relative impact, this does *not* mean that the words don't count. Words convey the content and meaning of your communication, while body language and voice give the content context. 'Context' includes deciding whether we believe what someone is saying or establishing how strongly they mean what they say.

Consider an example when the channels work together. You get off the plane after a long trip. Your partner is waiting for you as you step through into the arrivals hall. There's a loud shout of pleasure and they run towards you smiling, throw their arms around you, give you a warm kiss and say in an excited, happy voice, 'You're back! Welcome home – I missed you!' All the channels are in sync. You know your partner really is pleased to see you. If the body language and voice are consonant with the words, the words become incredibly powerful and we experience that person as being sincere.

But what if, instead of running gleefully towards you, your partner stands and waits for you to walk to them? They look down as you approach, not making eye contact. And when you reach them, they give you a quick peck on the cheek and say rather flatly, 'You're back. Welcome home – I missed you.' Chances are you'll start to feel quite anxious. Although the words are the same and still positive, the tone of voice and the body language aren't, and you're getting a mixed message.

Because of their low relative impact, the words can be seriously compromised when the body language and/or voice are 'out of sync' because, at 55% and 38% respectively, these two channels dominate and have greater relative impact. When you're on the receiving end of this clash, you experience a phenomenon called 'cognitive dissonance'.

When you're nervous or lying, you can undermine your messages by creating 'static', which helps to generate cognitive dissonance. This static can take the form of fidgeting with buttons, jewellery or hair, inappropriate smiling, a tremor in the voice, sweating and more. (These signals are sometimes called 'tells'.) The recipient of such 'message + static' can become uncomfortable, confused or even miss your message altogether. Of course, when you're making a big ask you might well be nervous and do any of the above.

All this means you need to manage your communication channels effectively and sync them up. Specifically, you must:

- Ensure you convey the right impression for your purpose and in a way that makes the prospect feel comfortable. This relates to Tool 2: Establish your personal brand in Chapter 1.

- Adapt your words, voice and body language to create a feeling of comfort and security with the prospect you're trying to engage.

We're going to focus here on the second element.

Let your body talk: The 3Ms of rapport building

Since body language carries 55% of the message in any face-to-face communication, it's clearly the major component in building rapport. With 38%, voice is not far behind. Going back to the dinner party example at the start of this section, the words that might have started the conversation, 'What do you do for a living?' or 'This red wine is lovely – have you tried some?', are important – they provide the *content*. We often try to use these questions to build rapport – we're actively looking for commonality, for connection. The way you use your voice – whether a quiet reflective tone or an excited high energy one – is also important because it conveys the mood. But the channel that outweighs both of them in the way the interaction is received is your body language. We often try too hard to build rapport simply through words and especially questions. Of course, it's good to look for similarity and connection verbally, but we also need to look for opportunities to build commonality with the other person's body language. We do this naturally of course – you can see two people who are relaxed and in rapport standing in a similar way. And of course when people are angry they will tend to raise their voices to a similar level and even make the same pointing gesture. There's a neurological basis to all this – see the section 'Rapport, empathy and mirror neurons' below.

It's helpful to distinguish the three different levels of activity in seeking commonality and connection that are often confused. Two are good and one is very bad. They are:

- mirroring

- matching

- mimicking

Let's begin with the two good ones:

Mirroring

Have you ever found yourself enjoying a conversation with someone, then noticed that you've unconsciously adopted broadly similar physical positions – for example, leaning back and laughing at a comment at the same time or picking up drinks in parallel? This is known as mirroring, and it is the equivalent of taking a series of behaviour 'snapshots' – aspects of another person's body posture – and then approximating them.

You can see examples of unconscious mirroring all around you. Next time you go into a bar or restaurant, take a moment to spot the people who seem to be getting on well. Chances are it's the fact that they are sitting in similar positions or using their hands in a similar way that leads you to that conclusion. They are mirroring each other's body language. Mirroring is a good thing, but it's a very basic way to try to build rapport.

Matching

Matching is the full-colour, 3D, real-time 'movie' version of building rapport – no 'snapshots' here. Sometimes called pacing, matching draws on body language *plus* voice and words. It involves getting broadly in sync with another person's movements, rhythms, language and gestures. Because you're using all three channels, the impact is richer and stronger. And because you're not exactly copying all that they do, the effect is more subtle.

Again, it's important to stress that matching is a natural process – it's something we do unconsciously all the time. And like mirroring, we're often completely unaware of what we are doing. When you're standing talking to someone, have you found you both start to gesture at the same time, and even to make the same kinds of gestures? (For example, using a chopping motion with one hand into the other to reinforce points.) Have you ever spent time with someone who has a distinctively different way of speaking from you – maybe their intonation rises at the end of sentences – and found yourself coming closer to their cadence? And have you found the words or phrases you use said back to you by other people when you're with them? What you – and they – have been doing is matching each other.

Below, we explore how you can become excellent at matching. Observe it in action and you'll soon notice how common it actually is. Skilled TV chat show hosts often use matching techniques to build rapport with guests. (Notice how Graham Norton often adjusts his voice and speech pace to match that of the person he's interviewing.) They do this to persuade the guest to 'open up' about their lives and careers more easily. Notice also how hypnotists get people into a 'trance' state by matching their body language, voice tone, breathing and even blink rate.

Mimicking

Mimicking is *exactly* copying every aspect of someone's body language. We don't, under any circumstance, recommend that you do this when you're trying to get in rapport with anyone – least of all a prospect. The literal copying of body language will be obvious and make the other person uncomfortable.

For example, you might find yourself copying a posture or voice tone that doesn't fit with your gender, sexuality or culture. It's good to kiss someone on the cheek three times in the Swiss style when you're there, or to use a formal bow when you're in Japan, where that's more appropriate.[4] But don't try to adopt a Scottish accent with your Scottish prospect if you're not Scottish. That said, when we're coaching people we often start by asking them to 'mimic' each other's body language. It helps them to notice just how much data is transferred in non-verbal communication. This might be useful for you too. We've found that some individuals are very good at matching upper body posture but fail to notice huge amounts of lower body activity, such as a tapping foot used to emphasise a point. Use mimicking to *learn* but not to build rapport in real life.

What can you match?

When you match, you're choosing to identify and build rapport through a selection of the other person's behaviours. The real skill is to identify those behaviours that make the biggest (unconscious) impact on the other person in terms of conveying commonality and similarity.

Below, we go through some of the main body language clusters you could match to make the communication easier.

- *Posture* – for example, leaning forward or backward in a chair and with crossed or uncrossed legs. Some people also lean forward to make a point.

---

[4] There are special challenges in matching body language across gender. Men, for example, will often sit with their legs spread apart. Women in Europe and North America tend not to do that as it's seen as 'unfeminine'. If they match this particular male body language, they are likely to come across as mimicking. In other cultures, however, it's entirely acceptable. In Kenya, you often see women in traditional long, flowing dress sitting with legs akimbo, appropriately matching the man.

- *Body movement* – for example, the amount of movement while speaking. Some people stay very still while some move a lot.

- *Gestures* – for example, there are lots of types of hand gesture: some people 'draw' pictures with their hands when they're talking while others make chopping or pointing gestures to emphasise words.

- *Touching* – for example, some people touch themselves, especially on the chest, for emphasis – this is called a 'disclosure' gesture. Some people like to touch objects – for example, play with a pen as they talk.

- *Facial expression* – for example, movements such as smiling, grimacing, eyebrow flash, and so on. Be careful, though, because some business people, lawyers, even foundation officers have learned to look 'neutral'.

Matching voice

Many people are aware of the importance of body language, but voice is often ignored – even though it's up to 38% of the relative impact of any communication. Voice matching is particularly important when you're working on the telephone – arranging a solicitation meeting, for example. As with body language, there are a number of elements to consider in voice:

- *speed* – the rate at which words and sentences are said

- *timbre* – the resonant qualities of the voice

- *volume* – the loudness or quietness of what is said

- *tone* – the 'brightness' of the overall voice

- *stress* – where the emphasis is in the sentence or phrase.

Voice varies considerably across cultures. For example, in general Spanish speakers – especially from northern Spain – tend to speak very quickly, whereas Nordics – especially Finns – have a relatively slow speech rate with lots of pauses.

Matching language style

You may have noticed that when people speak, they tend to use certain kinds of words more often. These seem to reflect the preference they have for processing information – visual, auditory or kinaesthetic (feeling).

As a successful fundraiser, you will notice these linguistic preferences and be able to adjust your own language style to match them. Unless you're one of the rare individuals who can do this incredibly easily and naturally, we suggest you start by preparing some key messages in each of the styles. (See Tool 16: Match language style – switch sensory systems later in this chapter for more on this.)

Top tip: Times to avoid rapport

Since rapport is a sense of connection with someone else, you will find there are occasions when you don't want to be in rapport:

- when the attentions of a potential supporter are inappropriate – they invite you out for dinner or a drink, then make it clear the purpose is not philanthropic business

- when the views being expressed are offensive and unacceptable – maybe sexist or racist – and you need to signal very clearly that you disagree

- when the support or 'deal' you're being offered by the sponsor or donor is unacceptable or unethical. You need to walk away from such situations.

In these cases and others, it's important to be able to break rapport quickly – and to send a message to the other person that they need to change their behaviour.

Rapport, empathy and mirror neurons

When researchers first began to study the process of rapport, they described it in quite behaviourist terms – 'This seems to work, it's not important why it works, just do it.' Now, though, we've come to understand that there is a neurological basis underpinning rapport – and empathy – connected to what are called *mirror neurons*.

In the 1980s, Italian neuropsychologist Giacomo Ritzzollati and his team conducted a series of experiments that have proved enormously influential in the neuroscience field. The scientists had placed electrodes in the brains of macaque monkeys looking to study the neural activity when the monkeys did various activities, including picking up and eating food. During the study, they discovered something unexpected. The same neurons[5] that fired in the same sequence in a monkey when it picked up and ate food also fired when it saw a human researcher pick up and eat a banana.

This and a number of subsequent studies led to establishing the existence of mirror neurons – neurons that exist not just in monkeys, but in people too. Essentially, these neurons drive a process that means when we see someone doing something, we experience whatever it is at some level ourselves. This means we can experience empathy in many situations. If we see someone fall, we may feel a similar anxiety and even say 'Ouch!' Or if we see someone eat a banana, we may be able to bring to mind the taste and feeling of a banana (and possibly want one too). Building physical rapport promotes empathy – to you *and* your message.

Neuro-linguistic programming: Why do some professionals succeed more?

In the early 1970s, two academics at the University of Santa Cruz began a study of professionals who were outstandingly

---

[5] The neuron is the basic working unit of the brain. It's a specialised cell designed to transmit information to other nerve cells, muscles or gland cells. See the discussion on anchoring in Chapter 1. An anchor is essentially a set of neurons firing together.

successful in their chosen careers – salespeople, lawyers and therapists. John Grinder, a linguistics professor, and Richard Bandler, an undergraduate specialising in computer programming, were interested in what made these professionals truly excellent. Their question was, 'Why, with the same qualifications and experience as their peers, do some professionals achieve significantly better results – greater sales, higher acquittals, more "cures"?'

Bandler and Grinder interviewed and videotaped their subjects. The research established that – unconsciously or consciously – they used a number of the techniques discussed elsewhere in this chapter. For example, they were good at building rapport through body language and voice. But for these individuals to be as successful as they were, there had to be some additional level of skill.

Eventually, the researchers identified the additional skill from a detailed linguistic analysis of transcripts of videos they made of their subjects in action. Their analysis showed that the successful subjects didn't only match the body language and voice of the person they influenced; they also changed their own spoken language to match as well. It was this extra factor that made the difference. From this initial discovery, Bandler and Grinder developed a body of work now called neuro-linguistic programming (NLP).[6]

---

[6] *Neuro* refers to the idea that the way we gather and interpret information is a function of neurological (brain) processes – taste, touch, smell, feeling, sight and hearing. Although everyone uses all of these to some degree, most people have a clear 'hardwired' preference for one or two.

Linguistic refers to the fact that our language – the frequency with which we use specific kinds of words and phrases – gives a clue to the preferences we have for this neurological processing. By listening

Put simply, NLP tells you that by paying attention to the words a person uses, you can gain essential information on how best to communicate with them and so 'translate' your message into their preferred language. Think of this as learning to speak Spanish when you go to Spain even though your first language is English.

A note of caution, however: NLP has, in our opinion, been oversold as a solution to a whole range of social, career, personality and mental health problems and challenges. In our view the linguistic flexibility element *is* a useful tool. We use it to coach fundraisers in high-level asks and in the design of case statements. You need to decide whether you want to take the rest on board. If you do, you might find the work of Sue Knight useful – see the booklist.

---

carefully to the kind of language someone uses, you can gain an insight into the way they think.

Programming is the idea that although individual *brain preferences* are hardwired, we *can* adapt. These adaptations are like mini-additions to the programmes in the brain's bio computer. Imagine you have a computer with PowerPoint but not Word. To read the Word document, you need to upload the right program. So having different preferences to your donor needn't mean you can't communicate successfully with them – you simply need to 'upload' their preferences.

Tool 16:
Match language style – switch sensory systems

When to use it: Use this tool if you're talking to someone and matching their body language and tone carefully and appropriately, BUT you still don't seem to be getting through. Try matching their language style. This is different to many of the other tools. You're not changing the message at all – just using different language to put it across.

Practice grade: 5

Bandler and Grinder's work established that individuals tend to use language that reveals their preference for how their brain gathers and processes information. These preferences are referred to in NLP jargon as sensory systems or sensory modalities.

Let's try an experiment to establish your preference (or preferences) for different sensory systems. Take a minute to think about a visit to a restaurant that you really enjoyed. Pause to recall a real situation for a moment and notice what comes to mind:

- Is it a picture of the beautifully presented food, the well-dressed waiting staff, the sparkling glasses and cutlery, and the different-coloured tea lights on each table?

or

- Is it the smell and taste of the food, the feel of the crisp ironed tablecloths, the comfortable chairs, and the pleasure of being in great company?

or

- Is it the choice of subtle background music, the great conversation among the party, the engaging description of dishes used on the menu, or the sound of food preparation from the kitchen?

You may have recalled all three. But most likely you remember one sensory experience much more strongly than the others. The strength of that recall provides an insight into your language preferences. (Even if they all appeared to be equal, the sequence in which they came to mind can help reveal a preference.)

Arising from the research was the discovery there are three main ways in which people take in, organise and express information – as pictures, feelings or sounds. In NLP-speak, these three primary sensory systems are called:

- *Visual* – perceiving and expressing ideas primarily in pictures, images, colours and shapes. Such a person might say, 'Show me some insight or clarification on your organisation's strategic focus. Where will my gift take us?'

- *Auditory* – perceiving and expressing ideas primarily through sounds and words. Such a person might ask, 'Can you just talk me through how your strategy speaks to the proposal you've suggested. Can you spell out how my gift will help?'

- *Kinaesthetic* – perceiving and expressing ideas primarily through feelings, touch, taste and smell. Such a person might say, 'I'm struggling a bit with how the proposal fits with your strategy. Can you help me get a handle on how my gift will push things forward?'

Bandler and Grinder's research showed that the 'added extra' their exceptional professionals had was the ability to unconsciously identify and match another person's language preference. Moreover, these high achievers were able to switch into another's language style quickly and easily, and it was this ability that was largely responsible for their exceptional level of success – completing the sale, winning over the jury, helping the client with therapy.[7]

It's important to stress that while most people have a preference for one of these systems when they're communicating, everyone can access all of them. Let's consider the three systems in a little more detail.

---

[7] Sometimes the system we favour is influenced by what we're doing or when we're doing it. For example, we're more likely to experience a painting *visually* in the first instance. But our response – or the way we *recapture* or *recall* that experience later – may reflect less about what was illustrated on the canvas and more about 'how it made us feel' or what the artist was 'trying to say'.

The visual person

If you primarily use the visual system, you notice first what you see. You organise and remember your thoughts in images or pictures. As you talk, you explain that you see challenges ahead, you plan to focus on priorities and you want to look at the big picture.

At a work meeting, you might notice the shape of the room, the mark a coffee mug has left on the table and the interestingly shaped earrings of the woman chairing the meeting. Afterwards, you can picture where people were sitting and how they were sitting – leaning away from or into the group – and the diagram someone drew on the whiteboard.

In a fundraising context, you may need to sketch out the priorities for the prospect, help them to get an overview of your organisation, look through some different options for future support and show them photographs of the new building being used by beneficiaries that their donation has helped to open. Notice here how the references are to interaction through images and pictures. When you explain things to a visual person, you may finish by saying, 'Do you see what I mean?'

The auditory person

If your primary system is auditory, you first take in and organise information by what you hear. You might find yourself replaying arguments or speeches in your head, rehearsing your responses to difficult donor questions and generally talking things over with yourself.

At a work meeting, you might find that the office noise outside the room makes it hard to concentrate and wonder where the person with the unusual accent is from; you only half hear the chair's summary of agreed action. Remembering the meeting, you may recall parts of the conversation verbatim and the tone of heavy sarcasm in the voice of one of your colleagues when they were asked to take a lead summing up the situation.

In a fundraising setting, you might offer to spell out the organisational priorities, to explain the case without using gobbledegook or jargon, to talk through different options for future support or to share written case studies where beneficiaries explain how they've gained from your help. Notice here that the references are to interaction through sounds and words. When you explain things to an auditory person, you may finish by saying, 'How does that sound?'

The kinaesthetic person

If your preference is the kinaesthetic – or feeling – system, you're likely to notice physical sensations when you first enter a room, such as the temperature and the smell – of air freshener if it's been used, or paper, or leather furniture. You may also be attuned to the emotional content of any situation. When you explain things, you talk about tackling the tough issues first, ironing out the poor bits of a presentation, working hard to get on with someone.

At a work meeting, you might notice how warm the room is and how uncomfortable the chairs are. Remembering the meeting, you may recall how frosty the discussion got at a particular point and how it made you feel on edge. But the pastries, you recall, tasted delicious...[8]

With a prospect, you'll stress that you know you're asking for a challenging gift, and that your cause has recently made some tough choices, and that beneficiaries responded warmly to the help the donor's generous donation provided. Notice here how the references are to interaction through feelings and images. When you explain things to a kinaesthetic person, you may finish by saying, 'Does that make sense?'

Working with language in a fundraising case

Later in this chapter, we deal with the issue of working with donors 'live' in a conversation or in a presentation. But to improve your skill in switching systems, you'll probably find it easier if you practise working on a written case – a formal explanation of your cause and need for money (see Tool 5: Build an =mc story arc and Tool 7: Price your philanthropic propositions in Chapter 2).

In our work with clients, we've used this language model to tailor donor-specific cases – or fundraising propositions. You can often find a video or audio of prospective donors making speeches or giving interviews. These are useful to

---

[8] Note: smell – *olfactory* and taste – *gustatory* are often included within the kinaesthetic system because they are both strong experiences that produce strong feelings. For instance, is there a smell from your childhood – such as your mother's perfume – which even just a whiff of today would bring back strong emotions for you?

identify preferences and key to rewriting your case to match their sensory preferences. The payoff is a proposition that's instantly more understandable and more acceptable to that prospect.

It's just as important and as respectful to translate your case into different sensory system preferences as it is to translate your case into Spanish or Chinese for non-English-speaking prospects.

When you're writing a general case aimed at a range of donors, you need to write it in a 'rich' way that uses all the modalities. Imagine a speech by a CEO to her charity's supporters at a fundraising gala written in 'unrich' language:

> I'm keen to be very candid with you. We've had some challenging returns against budget for the last financial period. And these have created some medium-term challenges for our services – especially with regard to those programmes that support young people at risk. These returns aren't just constraints on our cash flow. Ultimately, they impact on the financial viability of our helpline service. We're taking action to avoid unnecessary expenditure or to minimise it where practical. But we need your financial contributions too, or we may not be able to provide the service children and young people deserve.

Now imagine the same speech using the principles of richer communication:

> I have some news that's caused me and the rest of the team to lose a lot of sleep in recent months. Put

simply, I have to tell you we've made a significant loss in the last three months – income has fallen well below our fundraising budget. Those red numbers you can see at the bottom of the budget mean change. I've asked the team to tighten our belts in the next three to six months – to reduce expenditure where they can. But let me paint a realistic picture. If I can't sign the cheques to keep things going, that could mean phones ringing unanswered on the helpline. It means young people desperate to speak to a counsellor will be abandoned. I need you to join with us to make sure that doesn't happen.

Which of these speeches conveys the information more powerfully and emotionally?

 Top tip: Unequal preferences

Not all NLP language preferences are evenly distributed. Recent research suggests that:

- 35–45% of people have a predominantly visual preference

- 25–35% of people have a predominantly kinaesthetic preference

- 5–15% of people have a predominantly auditory preference.

According to other interesting data:

- there are no significant cultural differences worldwide – these distributions seem to hold in places as different as Africa and America[9]

- there are no differences in gender – women are not, as you might imagine, more kinaesthetic than men

- some professions have higher densities of particular styles – there are more auditory people in IT and finance.

How to notice a prospect's preference

Most people, including donors, don't communicate exclusively in one preference – what we're looking at or talking about, or getting a feel for… is frequency of specific kinds of language.

In Table 4.1 we've started a list of typical words and phrases that could provide you with cues for when someone is using each system. You should be able to add to it. Notice that you will probably find it easier to add to one or two of the columns because of your own preferences.

---

[9] We've used NLP in our influence and fundraising training in Ethiopia, Kenya, South Africa, Australia, New Zealand, United States, Canada, Mexico, Brazil, Argentina, Peru, Germany, France, Holland, Sweden, Italy, Thailand and Malaysia. It seems to work everywhere, and our own experience reinforces the general distribution data above.

Table 4.1: Typical words and phrases showing NLP preference

Visual system: Typical words	Auditory system: Typical words	Kinaesthetic system: Typical words
look; picture; focus; imagine; visualise; reflect; perspective; clarify; hazy; dim; colour	say; accent; ring; clear; discuss; remark; silence; tell; volume; sound; resonate; articulate	touch; handle; contact; rough; sensitive; stress; touch; grasp; bitter; smell; taste; impact
Visual: Typical phrases We see eye to eye I see what you mean You have a blind spot At first glance Looks pretty good to me Showing the way forward Future looks brighter	**Auditory: Typical phrases** On the same wavelength That rings a bell with me Listen to yourself talk A quick chat through Music to my ears Calling the tune Talking up the future	**Kinaesthetic: Typical phrases** Really connected That fits with my feeling You're stuck on that idea Scratch the surface Control yourself Sweet smell of success Feeling good about the future

Remember that everyone uses a mix from all the systems[10] – what you're looking for is a *preference*. An auditory donor will say more words or phrases from that cluster – giving you a clue to their preference.

---

[10] Some words and phrases don't really fit into this model either because they don't have a preference attached to them, or you can't identify one. Such language is called *digital*. Examples would be words like analyse, answer, communicate, remember, system, use. Also some phrases are simply clichés and don't reflect a real sensory choice. Examples might include 'I hear what you say' or 'Back to basics.'

How to quickly assess a prospect's preference upfront

You may be concerned that you'll find it hard to pick up a donor's preference face-to-face. Or at least that you'll find it hard to assess their preference and concentrate on the content of your message at the same time.

Fear not. The answer is to focus on discovering their preference before you get to the important part of the discussion. Use the 'ice breaking' time at the start of any meeting or phone call to good effect. Classic conversation openers like 'How are you?', 'How was your journey?', 'Did you have a good holiday?' and so on are not simply idle chatter. For the excellent influencer, it's a critical time for gathering key information about the prospect.

For example, when visiting someone in their house and being shown into their study, you can start a conversation by remarking, 'This is a great study!' Notice that their response will often take one of three forms:

- 'Thank you... I endlessly admire the view of the garden from here and I find I can bring real clarity to my thought.' (visual)

- 'Thank you... it's quiet here in the garden with just the birds singing and no traffic – so I can hear myself think.' (auditory)

- 'Thank you... I get the scent of the flowers when it's warm, and when I want a break a walk in the garden helps me to relax and sort out what's really important for me to get to grips with.' (kinaesthetic)

Even before you step into someone's office or home, you can pick up valuable information. Read an email they've written giving you instructions on how to find them. Again, you'll notice some differences in the way people give directions:

- 'We're opposite the bank on the corner. There's a car park entrance on the left, though you may have to look hard for a parking space. As soon as you walk back out of the car park you'll see our bright red 'Big Co' sign.' (visual)

- 'We're near a very noisy bar. Ask the parking attendant to tell you where there's a parking space if you have to. The words 'Big Co' are on the wall in red nearby – they caused a lot of comment when they were put up – that's where we are.' (auditory)

- 'It's not an easy place to find – and sometimes the car park is crowded. But everyone knows our offices and the red 'Big Co' sign is a sure way to guide you through the confusion. If you get lost, someone will help.' (kinaesthetic)

 Top tip: Other clues to language preferences

Apart from the words that people use, there are other clues to a person's preferences. For example:

- People who are visual tend to speak quickly, use a lot of gestures and breathe shallowly and in the upper part of their body.

- People who are auditory often have very even or melodious voices and breathe evenly with few gestures – though they often 'tap' in rhythm as they speak.

- People who are kinaesthetic are likely to speak more slowly, with pauses between ideas. They look down a lot as they speak and breathe from the bottom of their stomach.

Building up your own flexibility

It's easy to think of rapport-building as merely a way to get on the same communication level as people. But to be really skilful, and to build rapport generally, you need to be genuinely curious about people and work on your own flexibility. This involves not only noticing their preferences but also how and when (and in what circumstances) they change their preference. This curiosity about the channel is a powerful complement to the content. Being curious also helps you to take the time to check out that your idea or proposition has arrived with the prospective donor in the way you intended, and that they have fully understood it.

To be really successful when making a fundraising ask, you need to develop your flexibility with the approaches that are outside your own preference and be comfortable using them in 'live' situations. This is much the same as a top tennis player practising on different surfaces in order to adapt their game more readily to play on grass or clay. The secret, as always, is practice!

You can develop your flexibility in a number of ways:

- Listen to the radio or the TV carefully and with curiosity. Notice who speaks in one system almost exclusively and who swaps between them. Often people speaking 'off the cuff' – that is, taking part in live reporting or impromptu interviews where the interviewee is not choosing their words very carefully – can display a preference very strongly. See how quickly you can spot changes.

- Set yourself the exercise of translating the same speech with the same message to three people in an audience who each use one system exclusively. Imagine each is a commercial sponsor and you need to explain the benefits of supporting your charity concert. How might you share a benefit like brand awareness in one system at a time? ('Can't you just see your company name up there in lights?' 'Won't you feel proud at the connection of your company's logo with a joyful evening?' 'Can you hear the applause and people talking about what a great company you are if you support this cause?')

- Choose an object such as a car or a flower – or a fundraising technique such as a bequest or a direct mail. Without mentioning exactly what it is, describe its characteristics in one sensory system to someone, while they try to guess what it is. How difficult is it if you're not using your own preferred system? Was it easier for them to guess what it was when you used their preferred system?

Over time, you'll find that switching 'live' between systems becomes easier – but, as we've said, it takes practice.

 Action summary

✓ Look for opportunities to subtly prime your prospect in ways that will appeal to them and encourage them to think about your proposal in a more positive or open way.

✓ Begin by allowing the prospect to talk more – which means you need to be silent and listen more. If you are going to listen, do so with your whole body.

✓ When you want to build rapid rapport with someone quickly, complement their body language: pick up on the pattern of their gestures, and how they stand or move. Match these, where appropriate, and notice the effect this has.

✓ Make sure you match their language communication style – notice what type of words or phrases, or even ways of speaking, they prefer and work them subtly into your own communication.

Chapter 5

Persistence

Our greatest glory is not in never failing, but in rising up every time we fail.

Ralph Waldo Emerson

No matter how well planned and executed your ask, it may not work first time. People – especially potential donors or social investors – can be difficult to win round. You need to consider the fifth stage of our engagement process, *Persistence*, as key. This means believing so much in your idea, cause or proposition that you are prepared to try again after postponement or even refusal. Of course, there may be a point when you decide you need to walk away – but not until you've been through the tools we have to help you here.

In this chapter the four tools that ensure you really do explore every avenue to achieve success are:

- Switch points of view to help reframe a challenge using perceptual positions.

- Anticipate a big challenge by answering the killer questions.

- Seek advice from a team of experts who might help you – your mental mentors.

- Identify and respond to any of the nine 'no's that you're hearing.

Figure 5.1: The persistence power tools

Tool 17:
Pivot perceptual positions –
choose another angle

When to use it: This is another of these tools that you probably tend to use naturally. But here we're asking you to become more skilled and conscious in your use as a way to reflect and review on a situation so you can learn from it.

Practice grade: 2

In order to change someone's point of view, you first have to understand it. At the core of this is a powerful tool called *perceptual positions.*

We are all capable of experiencing the same situation from one of three perspectives, or 'positions':

- our own point of view

- the other person's point of view

- as a third party observing ourselves and the other person.

It's important to be aware of and able to spot these for several reasons:

- Each perspective has different advantages and disadvantages – and you can use them in different ways to achieve your result.

- By developing a skill in understanding and adopting the different positions, you'll quickly and easily be able to analyse the best perspective to win someone over.

- The three positions are also an excellent way to learn from a previous experience and review both how you did and how you could improve.

Positioning for fundraising influence

When you watch a film or TV drama, you're used to seeing the action from different points of view. Hitchcock is famous for this technique. In the famous shower scene in *Psycho*, for example, we see Janet Leigh's murder from all three perspectives: the third-party director/camera point of view to set the scene, the murderer's point of view and the victim's point of view. Added together, they make a truly terrifying 'experience' for the audience.

A less well-known example is *Vantage Point* (2008), a Pete Travis movie. Here we see the same event – the attempted assassination of President Ashton – through the eyes of eight different people. By taking this approach, Travis not only helps us understand the motivations of the characters at different points in the action, but also leads us to experience a moment of sympathy for an unattractive character when seeing the action through his perspective.

To be a successful fundraiser, it's essential you understand the prospect's point of view. This is more than being able to speak their language or empathise, which you learned to do in previous chapters. It helps if you can understand their partner's point of view, as well as that of their financial adviser, their children and anyone else who may be critical in the prospect deciding whether or not to support your cause.

When you're planning to make the ask, being able to switch between perceptual positions can open the door for you to:

- frame a fundraising proposition in a way that appeals to them in advance

- anticipate likely objections and prepare possible answers

- understand why people feedback in the way they do.

When you return to the office after the ask – whether successful or unsuccessful – being able to move between positions enables you to:

- make better use of any feedback or reaction you received

- recognise what you could have done better when reviewing what happened

- learn how to improve for the next time.

Choose your position

Below, we will describe three perceptual positions to consider when working with a prospect.

Position 1: The way you experience the world

In Position 1, you take in and prioritise information through your own eyes, ears and emotions. Position 1 (Figure 5.2) is important not just in terms of perception – it's also where you hold your values, beliefs and experiences.

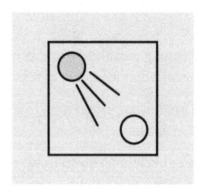

Figure 5.2: Perceptual position 1

Position 1 is where you create your emotional anchor (see Tool 1: Create a powerful emotional anchor) and where you set out your LIM-its (see Tool 10: Set out your LIM-its).

Advantages

By being clear about Position 1, you can:

- identify what exactly it is that you want in any given situation

- be assertive about your needs and interests.

Disadvantages

On the other hand, a perspective wholly based on Position 1:

- can come across as self-centred

- means you may not spot that the prospect isn't the slightest bit interested.

Position 2: The way someone else experiences the world

From Position 2 (Figure 5.3), you can step into the prospect's shoes and gain an insight into their perspective – their needs, values, experiences and desires.

Figure 5.3: Perceptual position 2

You might also appreciate and be able to share powerfully the point of view of the beneficiaries of the solicitation – for example, accurately sharing the feeling of isolation experienced by the young homeless person you are seeking funds to help.

Advantages

You should try going into Position 2 in order to:

- help you understand why you're not 'connecting' satisfactorily to someone

- identify why that person feels something is important to them that doesn't seem at all important to you.

Disadvantages

But you need to be careful with Position 2:

- You can identify too strongly with the prospect and their interests, losing your sense of self and holding back too much on your own interests.[1]

- You may get too involved in the perception of the *beneficiary* – in this case, the homeless person and their needs. You could then become over-emotional, losing your sense of perspective and possibly losing the prospect too.

Position 3: Observing the interaction from an objective 'external' position

In Position 3 (Figure 5.4), you step out from any internal perspectives – yours, the prospect's or the beneficiary's.

---

[1] In the worst case a fundraiser using Position 2 might back away from the solicitation because they sense this gift might cause a row between husband and wife.

William Ury[2] calls this perspective viewing from 'the balcony' – looking down on the action as an observer.

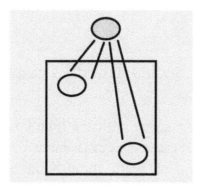

Figure 5.4: Perceptual position 3

This detached position lets you weigh up both points of view in a situation and maybe decide which has the stronger merit, or where a compromise goal might be reached.

It also allows you to act as the director in your mental movie, replaying a situation to think about alternatives in an unemotional and objective way.

Advantages

As a fundraiser at your best in Position 3, you may be able to:

- almost take 'time out' in the middle of a difficult meeting and assess how things are going – giving yourself advice on how to proceed

---

[2] William Ury, *Getting Past No* (1993).

- with practice, watch back the 'movie' review of what went well or less well in a prospect meeting and draw out some learning points for yourself.

Disadvantages

When Position 3 is less successful, a couple of things may occur:

- You may appear alienated from both your prospect and your cause. This can come across as world-weary cynicism, or 'going through the motions'. If you experience this jadedness, make sure you revisit Tool 1: Create a powerful emotional anchor and re-engage with your cause.

- If this is your preferred position, such detachment can mean you're unable to decide either way about an issue and come across as a little too distanced from feelings or emotions that are present and important.

You will probably find you have a preference for one of these positions – and so does everyone else. You need to be able to identify your prospect's (and any of their influencers'). And you need to be prepared to use all three positions in a single interaction if necessary to help identify or solve a particular challenge.

You should find it relatively easy to spot someone's preferred position in a specific situation. For example, you're talking to different prospects after an event, going over how it went from their point of view. You ask each one the same question: 'How was the gala fundraising dinner?'

- One says, 'I loved it from the minute I walked in. After a bit of a challenge finding my table I felt part of something really special. My meal was delicious – so many flavours to savour. Great to have a few friendly faces to greet me at the table. As soon as I heard the music I found myself up on my feet dancing with my partner in my arms. What a great evening.' (Position 1)

- Another says, 'I think I seemed a bit lost at first when I couldn't find my table. Certainly I got some odd looks from people as I pushed past. The server seemed pleased I cleaned my plate – but it looked like lots of people left food. My table companions made an effort to be friendly towards me – even though I was a bit on the edge of the action. When the DJ started the music, my partner made it clear I could not just sit there. What was good was that other people gave me some space to dance. They saw some of my best moves.' (Position 2)

- And yet another says, 'When I walked in everyone seemed to be having a good time, but I had to ask several people where my table was. I overheard a number of guests mentioning the food in a not very positive way, though I liked it. The music obviously had people excited. I wouldn't get up and start dancing first. But eventually I ended up in the middle of the dance floor strutting my stuff with my partner. Other people just had to get out of the way as I made some pretty good moves.' (Position 3)

This tool is another example where acuity is key. If you notice your prospect's preference in an informal conversation, it will help you to frame fundraising discussions. Notice that we're really only talking about important events with a high impact.

Deciding when to use each position

Different positions have uses in different situations. And it's interesting to note from a behavioural science point of view that people tend to use position 1 in the present as they think about the actions, but think about themselves in position 3 in the far future – as if they were someone else.

Position 1 is excellent for:

- Being assertive and making sure you stay calm under pressure – for example, before you go into a potentially difficult meeting rehearse how you might answer the particular concerns of a challenging prospect.

- Setting an outcome – Position 1 is a good place from which to tackle 'What do I want in this situation?' questions (see Tool 9: Develop a well-formed outcome in Chapter 3). For example, when you're negotiating with a commercial sponsorship prospect and want to ensure you don't concede too many benefits.

Position 2 is excellent for:

- Reassuring the prospect that you understand their situation – for example, someone who's nervous about the size of gift. This empathy will often gain you credibility with them. It also helps your oxytocin to flow.

- Assessing how the prospect might respond to some challenging news about the project – maybe that the cost has escalated and you need more support. Again, feel the oxytocin.

Position 3 is excellent for:

- Dealing with polarised situations – for example, after an especially tense prospect meeting when uncomfortable things were said and you need to get back on an even keel before you go back home to meet your partner or move to the next meeting.

- Reviewing a situation you think you handled badly – for example, considering how you might have better managed a solicitation that seemed to go off track, with the prospect appearing negative and you speaking irritably. Is that really what happened? Or not? And if yes, what could you have done differently?

Choosing the best 'position' for making the ask

As a fundraiser, it might seem obvious that you most often want to encourage donors to adopt Position 2 – and specifically the perspective of the charity's beneficiaries – so that they can appreciate how important their donation is to the people directly affected. Position 2 has some advantages, but it isn't necessarily the best.

Let's work through a fictional case study. WaterforLife is a non-profit organisation that works with people in rural Africa running sanitation projects. By doing this, it helps to protect the health and the safety of women and girls. It also removes from young girls in a community the burden of fetching and carrying safe water. The WaterforLife fundraiser needs to convince a prospect of the importance of the new local clean water pump project.

She might start by putting the prospect into a Position 1 perspective as they think about the life of a beneficiary. How would it have felt for them?

Thank you so much for all your generous support over the years. Today I'm asking you to consider contributing to our village water pump programme to help almost 6000 children living in Northern Uganda. Among them is Hilda. She's just 10 – the same age as your own daughter, Joanne. I'd like you to think back to when you were 10 and compare your normal day with Hilda's. Hilda gets up at 5.30 am when it's still dark to walk 6.5 kilometres along a dusty track to the nearest pump in the next village. There she fills two 11.5 litre jerry cans – like the ones I have here – to provide clean water for her mother and four little sisters. My guess is that when you were 10 you, like me, were woken by your mother way after 5.30 to tell you breakfast was ready. I guess too that the heaviest weight you had to carry each day was your school bag, and the longest distance was to and from the school bus. Hilda carries her jerry cans a total of 26 kilometres a day.

Hilda, along with many other girls like her, misses out on the start and end of every school day – cumulatively missing huge chunks of education. And she has little time to play – something essential to healthy child development and something you and I took for granted.

Alternatively, the fundraiser could frame the proposal in Position 2:

> Thank you for meeting me – and for your previous generous support to WaterforLife. I know you've seen the report from our field staff detailing how much your help has meant. Now they've asked me to ask you to help with the village water pump project. I'd like you to imagine you are Hilda, living in a small village in Northern Uganda. You are 10 years old. Every morning you rise in the dark at 5.30 to walk 6.5 kilometres along a dusty track to the nearest clean water pump in the next village. There you fill two 11.5 litre jerry cans. You balance one on your head and carry the other. Stopping frequently to change hands, you walk the 6.5 kilometres back home. You do the same after school. You'd love to be able to play with your friends, but you're always too tired. And anyway, it's getting dark again by the time you're finished.
>
> How do you imagine Hilda feels spending four hours each day collecting water? How do you imagine her life might change if she could be in school the whole day? And play with her friends?

Using Position 2, the fundraiser is asking the prospect to experience what it's like to *be* Hilda – to empathise with her world. Once there, they might be in a much better place to give – and to give generously. Our experience suggests if you have a prospect who can move into Position 2, you'll find it a very powerful place from which to fundraise. It's almost always worth trying to see whether the prospect connects. To help with this, make sure you also match the donor's preferred visual, auditory or kinaesthetic modality.

Interestingly, some donors prefer to commit from Position 3 – just as some people talk about themselves in the third person in their LinkedIn profile. Let's assume the WaterforLife fundraiser is meeting a different prospect. She knows he struggles to 'walk in another person's shoes' and his own comfortable lifestyle is worlds away from Hilda's experience. So she takes a different approach:

> Thank you for all your support in the past. I want to share a case study with you and to find out if you could see yourself making a difference. The case is about Hilda and 6000 other children like her in Northern Uganda. Here's a picture of Hilda, her mother and four younger sisters in their small village. Every day before dawn her mother has to wake her and ask her to make a 13 kilometre round trip to collect water for the family, carrying two heavy jerry cans. She does the same at the end of the day. I guess, like me, you would love to be able to step in and help Hilda with those heavy jerry cans. In the case study, which I'll leave with you, Hilda explains that this makes it hard for her to get to school on time. It also means she has to leave early to fetch water before it gets dark. Her teacher is concerned, of course, but recognises that Hilda has to help her mother. You can

see how Hilda, her mother and the teacher are all stuck and unable to make progress. Think how great it would be if there was a pump in the village, and one day you and Hilda were able to draw the first litre of water – just metres from Hilda's house. Hilda would get to school on time and would even have time to play with her friends after school – so essential for rounded child development.

We'd like you consider helping Hilda and the thousands of children like her. Imagine seeing yourself giving her the gift of childhood. Imagine being able to tell her she doesn't have to get up to fetch the water – and then listening to the family chatter when she eats breakfast with her mother and sisters. And how do you imagine Hilda's life would improve if she could join her teacher and classmates for the whole of the school day?

The fundraiser is asking the prospect to step into Position 3 to look at the world of Hilda, her mother, sisters and teacher from the outside in. And she's asking the prospect to put himself in the picture. Implicit in this view is a comparison with his own comfortable circumstances. Once the prospect is in this position, he might be better placed to understand – and, like the donor in Position 2, to give generously.

As you read these scenarios, you might well find yourself thinking one is obviously 'better' than the others. But they're not – they're all just different. And you probably have a preference for the one that matches your own preferred position.

Tool 18:
Anticipate killer questions

When to use it: All causes have issues that don't reflect well on them, their staff or their programmes. (Think of the damage sexual scandals did to Oxfam and governance challenges to Amnesty in recent years.) You can't pretend that these 'scandals' didn't happen. And you need to be ready to answer any challenges – the killer questions – if you're asked. They're really only killers if you can't answer them.

Practice grade: 1

The feared but reasonable killer question is the one you have been dreading. It's the flaw in your case you know exists. Or it's the challenge about your organisation's work you hoped would not be raised. You fervently hope the person you're trying to win over won't ask it. But what if they do? You have to have a response.

Killer questions can take a range of forms:

Scandal

Every organisation has, or has had, its scandal or scandals. (If you don't know about the ones in your organisation, it's because you haven't been paying attention or haven't been there long enough.) There are times when scandal can almost bring the organisation down, as in the Oxfam and UNICEF sexual misconduct scandals. Some 'scandals' may not be true or only partly true. The media – mainstream and social – will as happily share an unsubstantiated rumour as they will exaggerate limited facts. Make sure you check your organisational skeletons and that you're familiar with:

- the facts – as well as the misinformation that has been shared

- how this issue was/is being dealt with

- how you will respond to a challenge about it.

Crisis management

Even if your organisation doesn't have a scandal at the moment, and hasn't had one in the recent past, is there a potential one that might emerge – a problem that could expand into a crisis without proper advance contingency planning? (Such events are sometimes called Black Swans – 9/11 or Covid-19 type events that apparently emerge from nowhere.) The crisis could be financial, or it could be to do with waste or abuse. Again, have you prepared an answer or a strategy to deal with this?

Showing that you have proactively developed policies to mitigate such risks helps. Supporters or prospects can be understanding provided they can see you haven't been hiding information and are trying to behave properly.

Poor benchmark

Maybe the thing you'd most like to keep hidden is how you compare with other agencies. Perhaps you spend more on administration than other comparable organisations, or maybe your service or artistic record is poor compared with that of your main rivals. How will you deal with this if the donor is aware of it? One way is to put a better spin on the figure or comparison that's being used. ('It's true we're more expensive, but the quality of our work is better.') Another way is to acknowledge that you don't compare so well, and to adopt Avis's 'We try harder' approach. You might actually gain some credibility by the admission and could, if you played it right, win an advantage. (Remember the importance of the pratfall effect, discussed in Chapter 2.)

 Top tip: Learn from others' mistakes

In 2013, the global environmental campaign group Greenpeace fired an employee after it discovered he had lost some £3.5 million of its money in a 'bet' on international currency markets.

The official explanation was that the loss was the result of a 'serious error of judgement' from an individual in the group's international finance unit, who 'acted beyond the limits of their authority and without following proper procedures'. Of course, almost every international charity and international business does such currency hedging. (And a number of charities have lost – and gained – money in this way.) But this example, now fixed of course, made it sound like there weren't robust procedures in place. And that could make a prospect anxious – stirring up hygiene factors. As recently as 2017, we discovered one of our very large consulting clients had a similar 'scandal', amounting to some hundreds of millions of dollars, that was known about internally but simply hadn't emerged publicly. We worked hard to help them develop an explanation in case it did.

You may also remember the Vilar Scandal. Alberto Vilar was a New York-based investment adviser famous for his love of opera. In 2005, as his wealth reached £4.3 billion, he made charity pledges of about £128 million to music, education and health causes worldwide, from the American Academy in Berlin to the Los Angeles Opera. But he was able to pay only half of them after his investment fund crashed.

Worse still, it emerged that much of the money he had committed as a philanthropist wasn't actually his but belonged to his clients. He was arrested and sent to jail for a range of fraud and money laundering crimes. But then many organisations, including the UK's Royal Opera House, had the problem of what to do about the fact they had taken money that technically belonged to Vilar's clients, and what to do about buildings or programmes associated with him. Pay it back? Keep it? Remove his name from the list of benefactors of the building?

This is really what's technically called a *wicked problem* – there *is* no good solution after the event. Of course, the learning is to have an ethical screening policy. But Vilar's perfidy was hard to know about upfront, and he passed lots of the screenings for a number of agencies worldwide. Be ready for the unexpected!

Tool 19:
Call your mental mentors –
ask for help

When to use it: Let's say you really need some personal advice to help you deal with a situation. Maybe you need to talk through a difficult situation coming up. Why not call on the top coaches who could help you?

Practice grade: 3

You almost certainly have people you admire for specific qualities. They may be real people you know or celebrities. They may be historical or even fictional. These people inspire you because of their calmness under pressure, or their perseverance, or their ability to think ahead. Wouldn't it be great if you could seek help or advice from these people whenever you needed it – if you had a team of mental mentors? The good news is that you can.

Our inspiration for this tool comes from Hillary Clinton,[3] former US secretary of state and 2016 presidential candidate.

---

[3] You've probably heard the phrase, 'What would Jesus do?', often presented as an acronym, WWJD. This is a similar idea to one popularised by Christians, originally in the United States in the late 1800s. It's claimed that it came from a book by Charles Sheldon, *In His Steps: What Would*

In her autobiography she talks about the importance of the mentors who helped in her early career.

During her husband Bill's term of office as president, Hillary had some difficult situations to deal with. She was keen to make sure she thought them through before taking action. Her husband was often busy or away on diplomatic trips. And, of course, there was a time when she couldn't trust him or many of the White House staff. To help her, she invented 'mental mentors' – virtual individuals whose advice she could trust. She would find herself a quiet space and imagine she was in discussion with two or more people. She would pose some questions on what course of action she should take and imagine them advising her on what to say or do. The mentors allowed her to think through the same questions in different ways, opening up different alternatives from which to choose.

This technique is useful for tackling a whole range of work and personal challenges. You'll find it particularly applicable to fundraising asks when you're not sure how to proceed. Of course, you almost certainly want to have some fundraisers as mentors. Think about the people you most admire and add them to your list.

In our own practice, we have collected a group of mental mentors to advise us on everything from tactics, to choice of language, to PR initiatives. Of course, the answer really comes from you – or at least from your unconscious. But it's

---

Jesus Do? The phrase and idea regained popularity in the 1990s as a way of resolving a moral or social dilemma faced by Christians.

a useful discipline to think about who you would seek advice from and what advice they would offer. It can even give you permission to think the unthinkable.

Table 5.1 gives you a list of possible areas for coaching and the kinds of figures – historical and contemporary, real and fictional – who might be able to help. You can also use people from your own life of course.

Table 5.1: Areas for advice and possible mentors

Area for advice	Who might mentor
What to say that will move or inspire	Martin Luther King, Greta Thunberg, Shakespeare's Henry V
How to recover from a setback	Thomas Edison, anyone from the crew of Apollo 13, Mulan
What to wear for a specific situation	Paul Smith, Stella McCartney, Donna Karan
How to develop self-confidence	Hermione Granger (from Harry Potter), Alexander the Great,[4] Bill and Melinda Gates
How to stay calm and patient	The Dalai Lama, Nelson Mandela, Charlotte Bronte's Jane Eyre

Three things about your list are particularly important:

1. Choose people who you genuinely believe you can imagine speaking to you. Give them a voice. To present you with real choices, they need to appear real to you in your head – probably sitting opposite you at a table.

2. Make sure you choose people you respect, but they needn't necessarily be people you like. Some of our

---

[4] Alexander the Great? Well, when he started forging his great empire he was just 21, gay in a very macho society (remember, he was Macedonian by birth, not Greek) and had no maps of the places he wanted to conquer. What's your challenge…?

best advice has come from an imaginary Margaret Thatcher – a person neither of us liked politically, but who did display great clarity of purpose at various times.

3. Don't feel you need to select people who will agree with one another. In fact, it can be useful to have access to people who might disagree. That then allows you to weigh up more options effectively. Remember, this is really a framework for you to consider different options.

Once you have the list for your mentoring/coaching group, here's how to use it:

1. Decide the question you want to pose. As ever, it's better to make it as specific as possible. Try to ask questions that might help improve on something: 'How should I challenge that volunteer's behaviour?' or 'What kind of metaphor or example would make the biggest impact with that donor?' You can also ask outcome-type questions – for example, 'What might be the advantages and disadvantages of writing a follow-up letter to the donor?' Don't ask 'yes' or 'no' questions. This isn't Luke Rhinehart's *Diceman*.

2. Assemble a selection of mental mentors who you think might be helpful for this specific challenge. Always have at least two and ideally three. Wise people can mentor in different areas. Note that your mentors don't have to be fundraisers – a businessperson might well be the best person to advise on how to influence another businessperson.

3. Find a quiet space with a comfortable chair where you can think, or fantasise if you like, uninterrupted for 15 to 20 minutes. Close your eyes and imagine your mentors sitting round a table advising you. Don't try to take notes while being coached.

4. Pose the question to each of your mentors and imagine their answer. Give them time to respond. Imagine them being physically present in the room offering advice. Focus on one mentor at a time. But after you've 'heard' the opinion of one mentor, it's useful to 'look' around the table at the other mentors and seek their views on the advice you've just been offered. In our experience, mentors don't always offer the answer straight away. If one mentor doesn't know the answer at all, try another. Stay open-minded until you've listened to all the responses.

5. Open your eyes. And, if appropriate, take notes on what you heard. If necessary, choose between the different options. Remember that they're only mentors. They're there to offer *advice*. It's ultimately your choice about what to do. In the end, you need to be your own ultimate mentor responsible for the final decision.

Tool 20:
Manage the nine fundraising 'no's

When to use it: Often you will get a rejection. But there are many different ways in which a prospect might say 'no'. And you need to learn to spot the different kinds and respond differently.

Practice grade: 1

People won't always agree with your initial proposal for support. In fact, they *often* won't agree. The reality is you are still likely to get a 'no' more often than a 'yes'. Beware hearing a definite 'no'. The difference between a successful and an unsuccessful influencer is that they rarely accept the first 'no' as a definitive answer. The successful influencer responds by being curious about what exactly the donor means.

There's Darwinian logic to this, at least in fundraising. Put simply, if you only asked people who would definitely say 'yes', or if you only asked for the size of donation that you were sure they would definitely give, you'd:

- be working off a very, very small sample of prospects

- probably tend to 'under-ask' by framing your proposition very low.

And worse, you could be letting down your cause and the people you're there to help.

To be successful as a fundraiser, you need to learn to deal with the possibility of rejection. And in particular you need to deal with initial rejection and be able to analyse it more closely. That first 'no' may not be as bleak as it initially appears.

To help you manage and interpret the possible rejections you might experience, we've created a 'no' typology. In our experience, there are essentially nine fundraising 'no's used by prospects. With the first eight of these, if you follow up with a better question you may well get a better result. Only one of these responses – the last one – genuinely means 'No, go away.' And if you hear this 'no', you should leave. But mind you still say 'thank you' to the prospect for their time – see the box below for the possible payoff for good manners.

The nine fundraising 'no's are:

1. No, not for this.
2. No, not you.
3. No, not me.
4. No, not unless.
5. No, not in this way.
6. No, not now.
7. No, too much.
8. No, too little.
9. No, go away.

Each of these 'no's has an underlying reason or explanation that a skilled influencer will seek to uncover. And that's why dealing with 'no' properly requires that you ask a different or better question rather than simply giving up.

Getting from no to yes

Table 5.2 explores our nine fundraising 'no's typology. In it we suggest why you might get a particular 'no', what the donor might really want from you and how you could respond in a way that might lead to a more positive outcome.

Table 5.2 The nine fundraising 'no's typology

No	Reason the donor gives	What is the donor really thinking – and how might you respond?
1. No, not for this	'You've asked me to support your education programme for children, and I'm not interested in work with children.'	'Why don't you ask me to support your work with adults or elders? I'm interested in that kind of work.'
		If you know they are interested in your work, what specific aspect would they like to support?
2. No, not you	'I'm not comfortable with you soliciting this gift.' (The solicitor is maybe a 30-year-old woman and the donor a man of 70+.)	'I'm 70 years old and want to talk to someone my own age who shares similar life experiences and understands how I feel about the importance of a legacy gift.' (Or I want to talk to someone of my faith, or with my sexuality…)
		Who's the right person to ask the donor – who will they feel comfortable with?
3. No, not me	'I'm not the right person to ask – I can't or don't make those decisions.'	'I don't make these decisions. You should talk to my partner – she decides about our charitable giving.' (Or you should talk to the marketing director if it's a company, or one of the other trustees who has an interest in this field if it's a foundation.)
		Who is the key decision-maker who will decide whether to back this proposal?

4. No, not unless	'You don't seem to be offering me what I need or want in return for my gift.'	'I need to have my deceased partner's name on this building as part of the gift fulfilment.' (Or 'No, unless you provide the following commercial benefits...' if it's a sponsorship.)
		What is it they really want and can you ethically or reasonably provide it?
5. No, not in this way	'You've asked me for cash and I can't help with that.'	'I could help with some other kind of support through my business interests, like vehicles, printing, and back office services, but you don't seem interested in other kinds of support.'
		If not money, how else can they help?
6. No, not now	'I can't help you at this time.'	'Why don't you ask me for a donation in a year's time after my daughter has graduated from university?' Or 'When I've sold the company.' Or 'Towards the end of our foundation financial year when we know what resources we have left'.
		When would be a good time to make this ask?
7. No, too much	'I can't give you that amount of money.'	'I don't have that sum available or it doesn't fit with my commitment to your cause. Ask me for a different – lesser – sum that will be meaningful for you and is within my range.'
		What sum might be appropriate, acceptable and still help with your project?

8. No, too little	'I want to do something bigger and more important, and that sum doesn't relate to that feeling or commitment.'	'Ask me for a different – larger – sum that will be meaningful for me and relates to my ability to give. I want to make what I perceive really is a significant difference or an impact.' What kind of sum is appropriate and can you use it properly?
9. No, go away	'No.'	'I've thought about your proposition and decided that it isn't what I want to support.' Say thanks and back away… Is the door permanently closed, or what might have to change for there to be a possibility of re-establishing the relationship?

In truth, there are probably more than nine 'no's, but these are a good start in that they force you to listen carefully and actively to the response – 'no' needn't be final.

It's especially important to try to work out which 'no' is being used when:

- You're in a live one-to-one situation where the initial rejection might seem to be the end of the conversation. It helps you look beyond your own immediate disappointed reaction.

- You're helping a colleague who's returned from an unsuccessful prospect visit and they need help to identify what else they might have done to recover a situation that was going wrong.

The hidden thinking behind 'no'

The tactics we've outlined are good behavioural responses to the 'no'. But there is a link to another element in the book that reveals some of the hidden or deeper processes behind a 'no' that can become a 'yes'.

No and chunking

The specific questions you ask to distinguish different 'no's link strongly to the chunking up technique That is, when you reach a block or challenge, you can scale an idea or concept 'up' – make it bigger – to find out where there is agreement. When someone says 'no' to your ask, you might chunk up with, 'Well, I'm disappointed you can't support our education programme but I'm guessing from what you said earlier you do feel the general principle of outreach work is a good one?' If the answer is 'yes' to this, then you've successfully chunked up and simply need to find an alternative outreach programme for the donor. If the answer is still 'no' when you chunk up to outreach, you may want to consider asking a more general chunk-up question, 'What was it that first attracted you to our cause?' Such a question might elicit an answer – 'Well, I really became involved because of my late husband's admiration for your CEO' – that takes you off in a completely different direction. And at that point you chunk down to find out what the donor's late husband was interested in.

The important thing about the nine 'no's is that you can generally plan for them and prepare an appropriate response or have a better – different – question ready.

We've come almost to the end of our five-stage journey – though remember that the point about the interlocking cogs is that you sometimes need to rewind to succeed. Of all of our stages, the one that will define your long-term success is undoubtedly your persistence – the ability and desire to persevere.

Here's our summary to help you keep up momentum.

 Action summary

- ✓ If you're not sure how to tackle a challenge, try to switch points of view using perceptual positions. Think especially about using Position 3 to analyse what you can learn from the situation, or to create a possible future if you had another chance.

- ✓ Learn to anticipate a big challenge in the form of killer questions. You need to have a list of these questions and your answers ready. Make sure you know about the scandals – real or imagined.

- ✓ Still not sure what to do? Then call on your ready and willing team of mental mentors – the world-class experts who can help you anytime, anywhere.

- ✓ Finally, don't lose heart when you hear what sounds like – and indeed might be – a 'no'. Instead, learn to identify and respond to the particular one of the nine 'no's you're hearing. Often 'no' means 'ask me a better question'.

Final summary...
and bonus tool 21:
Ask three questions

When to use it: This tool will help you to keep learning and improving. You need to be committed to systematic review and learning – what's called an *after-action review.*

Practice grade: 1

We hope the book has proved useful – and especially the five stages and 20 tools. All the tools are based on solid science and practice. But even so, as we've said several times throughout the book, people are 'messy' so there is no guarantee that any one approach will work.

No matter what the outcome, you can gain from any situation where you try something and are then prepared to learn from it. But you do need a systematic process for this learning.

We've developed a super-simple three-question approach for an after-action review – essentially a bonus, and final, tool. Use it after every proposal, every meeting and every call. We use these questions in coaching and consulting too.

The challenge very often is:

- If the solicitation goes well, you may start to rewrite history and imagine that you did everything well or that everything you did contributed to the success.

- If the solicitation goes badly, you may start to see the entire process as having gone badly, blaming yourself or even the prospect.

Use the following three questions instead. The questions are specifically sequenced to enable you to gain most from the review. They're designed to help you arrive at a sensible assessment of what actually happened – and identify what you should try to do next time. Find a quiet space and sit down with a pen and paper to answer these.

1. *What worked?* Begin by identifying what worked – that is, what was successful – even if the only thing that worked was that you turned up on time for the meeting. Make a list of the elements that worked and the techniques you tried. Begin with this list. Switch off the 'fella in the cellar' – the negative voice in your head that encourages you to begin with what went wrong.

2. *What didn't work?* Next (though, as we've seen, it's tempting to go here first), identify what didn't work. This a helpful second question, even when you were successful. Don't be afraid to list different-sized elements: big – 'I misjudged the potential value of the gift available' – and small – 'I was maybe a bit too informal at the start'. Do the same with the techniques you tried but that failed or didn't work properly.

3. *How could you improve?* Using the two lists you have compiled so far, consider how you could improve if you had to tackle the same situation again. You might find that the perceptual positions technique we

discussed in the last chapter is helpful here, looking at what happened from your point of view, from their point of view, and as an outside third-party coach. The third-party coach approach allows you to replay what happened as a mental movie, then play some alternative endings.

Build that learning into your next solicitation.

Books and online resources

Books

Fundraising

Ken Burnett, *Relationship Fundraising* (Wiley, San Francisco, 2002)

This is an outstanding work that revises and updates the original classic version of this book. It is essential reading for any fundraiser and explores the idea that fundraising needs to move beyond transactions to genuine relationships. You'll see evidence of Burnett's work everywhere there's good fundraising.

George Smith, *Asking Properly* (White Lion Press, London, 1994)

The definitive work on how language, and especially well-written copy, can transform your case into a powerful ask. Written by one of the leading figures in European fundraising, it distils his knowledge and experience into a readable volume. Indispensable for the serious fundraiser.

Bernard Ross and Clare Segal, *The Influential Fundraiser* (Wiley, San Francisco, 2008)

Our original work on how fundraisers can influence others – donors, board members, colleagues and more – and where we developed the 5P model and explored it in real-life situations. This current book builds on the learning from over 10 years of applying these techniques in a range of settings.

Rapport

Michael Argyle, *Bodily Communication* (Methuen, London, 1992)

A comprehensive introduction to an overview of the field of non-verbal communication and how it relates to other forms of communication. The book has an academic outlook, but is very good at analysing behaviour issues and not jumping to 'easy' conclusions.

Desmond Morris, *Peoplewatching* (Vintage, New York, 2002)

Morris is the definitive watcher of people, their behaviour and habits, personalities and quirks. This book explores how people consciously and unconsciously signal their attitudes, desires and innermost feelings with their bodies and actions. It is great for improving your cross-cultural awareness.

Negotiation skills

Roger Fisher and William Ury, *Getting to Yes: Negotiating Agreement Without Giving In* (Penguin, New York, 1991)

This is a short, practical, easy-to-read guide to the practice of what Fisher and Ury call 'principled' negotiation. This was developed from the Harvard Negotiation project, which studied how political negotiations could go wrong.

William Ury, *Getting Past No* (Bantam, New York, 1993)

Building on Ury's previous bestselling work *Getting to Yes*, this book offers helpful advice on handling the negative side of negotiation – staying in control under pressure, refusing anger and hostility, finding out what the other side really wants and countering dirty tricks.

Gavin Kennedy, *Everything is Negotiable* (Random House Business Books, New York, 2008)

Very business/consumer-orientated in the examples used, but offers useful advice. There are self-assessment tests at the start of each chapter, which Kennedy answers at the end of the chapter with a suggested score. Other features include a helpful mail service for readers, five negotiating scenarios and a two-hour MBA-level negotiating exam.

Neuro-linguistic programming

Sue Knight, NLP at Work (Nicholas Brearley, London, 1995)

A clear and readable guide that explains the terminology and provides advice on how NLP techniques can be put to practical use.

Kevin L. Johnson, Selling with NLP (Nicholas Brearley, London, 1999)

This is a useful, practical book that takes key elements of NLP and shows how to use them in commercial sales environments. The link to influence and fundraising in not-for-profits is relatively easy to make.

Behavioural science

Dan Ariely, Predictably Irrational: The Hidden Forces That Shape Our Decisions (HarperCollins, New York, 2009)

Why do smart people make irrational decisions every day? Dan Ariely cuts to the heart of our strange behaviour, demonstrating how irrationality often supplants rational thought. He combines everyday experiences with psychological experiments to reveal the patterns behind human behaviours and decisions.

Phil Barden, Decoded: The Science Behind Why We Buy (Wiley, New York, 2013)

Barden's book uses decision science to explain the motivations behind consumer choices and shows how this can be valuable to marketing. Although there are few not-for-profit examples, the learning from commercial marketing is easy to apply. Barden deciphers the 'secret codes' of products, services and brands to explain how they influence our purchase decisions.

Bernard Ross and Omar Mahmoud, *Change for Good: Using Behavioural Economics for a Better World* (SemiosCreation/=mc publishing, 2018)

Drawing on a decade of research in behavioural economics, neuroscience and evolutionary psychology, this book provides a powerful yet practical toolkit for everyone from fundraisers and campaigners to policy-makers and educators. It offers advice on how to raise more funds or help people improve their diets, showing how techniques commonly used in commercial settings can be adapted to social good, including engaging supporters.

Daniel Kahneman, *Thinking, Fast and Slow* (Macmillan, New York, 2011)

Nobel Prize-winning thinker Kahneman explains how two 'systems' in the mind make decisions. One system is fast, intuitive and emotional; the second is slower, more deliberative and logical. They work together to shape our judgements and decisions. This book exposes both the capabilities and biases of fast thinking and reveals the pervasive influence on our thoughts and behaviour.

Robert Cialdini, *Pre-Suasion: A Revolutionary Way to Influence and Persuade* (Simon & Schuster, New York, 2016)

Three decades after writing his bestselling *Influence* book, with its six key principles, Cialdini delivered a sequel that extends the classic work in several ways. He offers new insights into the art of winning people over – it isn't just what we say or how we say it that counts, but also what goes on in the key moments before we speak. Cialdini reveals how to master the world of 'pre-suasion', where subtle turns of phrase, tiny visual cues and apparently unimportant details can prime people to say 'yes' before they are even asked.

Online resources

www.mc.consulting/makingtheask

This is the website linked to the book. Here you can find a host of additional resources to help you make the perfect ask. These include:

- case studies
- worksheets
- quizzes
- more detailed explanations of the 20 tools
- more tools!
- webinar opportunities
- training opportunities

... and more. You can even ask questions of the authors, Clare Segal and Bernard Ross.

www.decisionscience.org.uk

This website provides a portal to the latest thinking and practice on decision science and how it can help in fundraising and more. Again, you can find:

- case studies

- downloads

- video tutorials, etc.

https://sofii.org – Showcase of Fundraising Inspiration and Insight (SOFII)

SOFII is an amazing global portal and archive, which documents the very best in fundraising practice worldwide. It is full of amazing examples of campaigns and case studies of fundraising successes and failures. Not many are directly connected with making the ask, but there are some great ideas about direct mail online and other forms of solicitation that might provide insights and inspiration for you.

Training, consulting and coaching

Our company, =mc consulting, runs training programmes in solicitation skills for fundraisers and for other non-profit leaders internationally, based on the *Making the Ask* framework. We also coach individuals and teams. Among the agencies and individuals we have helped to make high-level asks are:

- *Diane Fossey Gorilla Fund.* We coached the then president of DFGF protecting the last 700 gorillas in the wild to make successful $1 million+ solicitations to several HNWI in the United States, including the billionaires Ted Turner and Larry Ellison.

- *KidsOR.* This organisation aims to build a paediatric surgical unit and train surgeons, nurses and anaesthetists in every African nation. They need $100million in the next five years from major donors especially in Africa – we developed the case.

- *UNHCR MENA.* This specialist team, based in Dubai, has to raise $300 million+ every year across the Middle East to meet the growing needs of refugees. We combined *Making the Ask* ideas with Islamic philanthropic principles to help.

- *British Heart Foundation.* We coached the chair and volunteer board of this major UK health charity to improve their ability and confidence to ask wealthy peers for their financial support.

- *Stonewall.* This campaigning equality agency offered to train 20 leading Southern African LGBTQI activists in fundraising asks for a challenging cause. =mc consulting provided the skills.

- *IFRC.* We worked with the IFRC teams across the Asia-Pacific region to provide skills and confidence in seeking support for the Red Cross and Red Crescent's vital work from the growing number of Asian donors in China.

- *UNICEF UK.* The high-performing philanthropy team at UNICEF UK benefited from =mc consulting training in storytelling and making the ask – helping them to engage more and bigger donors.

- *World Animal Protection.* The WAP high-value team needed support to pitch to media mogul Simon Cowell as a potential sponsor through involvement in one of his TV shows. They won the deal.

- *US Olympics Association.* Like many sports associations, the US teams have to raise funds from corporations, foundations and individuals to grow talent. =mc consultants provided the frameworks.

- *Alzheimer's Association USA.* We worked with chapter and HQ teams of this research charity to help them secure more and larger gifts from donors, state by state. Over several months, we worked on their supporter journey and *Making the Ask* skills.

- *MSF International.* The major humanitarian agency brought together its face-to-face fundraising teams from across the globe to learn more about the psychology of street solicitation. =mc consulting provided the thinking.

- *University of Glasgow.* When this prestigious UK university launched its first £1 billion campaign, it needed the whole team to be confident in solicitation. Two days' training did that.

- *University of Oxford.* The HNWI solicitation teams across the Oxford colleges wanted some high-level insights into how to engage demanding major donors. We provided them using the *Making the Ask* framework and decision science.

We also develop powerful cases for support designed to win over prospects. We've done this for many of the agencies listed above and more.

Finally, we offer conference presentations in aspects of fundraising, communications and influence.

To learn more, contact us at www.mc.consulting or b.ross@managementcentre.co.uk or c.segal@managementcentre.co.uk

Additional resources – FREE!

To complement the book, we've created a website with a range of additional resources – videos, downloads, self-assessment sheets and more. To access these goodies for free, visit www.mc.consulting/makingtheask

Acknowledgements

Any book is a labour of love, and the love of many people is needed to bring it to fruition. We'd particularly like to thank…

Alison Jones, inspirational publisher, and top guru at Practical Inspiration Publishing. And her ever-on-it and helpful assistant Shell Cooper. Marina Jones, UK fundraising star, Head of Membership & Fundraising Campaigns at the Royal Opera House, London and brilliant critical eye. Toni Giddings for her wonderful and speedy design work on the tools that has added so much. Sophie Robinson and her team at Newgen Publishing UK for politely but firmly moving the process on. And last but by no means least, Susan Jarvis for her careful and thoughtful editing.